AMERICA'S RETIREMENT
REALITY CHECK

AMERICA'S RETIREMENT

REALITY CHECK

Yes ⬅ Retire? ➡ No

⬇

Not Sure?

NANCY & DAVID ELLIS

Printed in the United States

First Printing, 2015

ISBN-13: 978-1-4951-8290-7 (print)

ISBN-13: 978-1-4951-8291-4 (e-book)

JRE Publishing

Cover design and figures by Design at Work.

Interior design by Marisa Jackson.

TO ALL OF OUR

LIFE AND ANNUITY MASTERS FAMILY

TABLE OF CONTENTS

INTRODUCTION

I TURNED 50 THIS YEAR—50!—and here's the thing: I don't feel it. Fifty to me looks like my mom did at my age or my friends' moms—kids raised and living on their own, life slowing down a bit. They let their hair gray. They played golf. That's not my life.

First of all, four of our kids aren't even 10 years old. As for gray hair, I'm at the tail end of the boomers, the forever young generation—I'm dying my hair. Who has the time for a leisurely game of golf? I'm hitting the gym five days a week. And while I'm hauling myself to the gym, touching up my roots, driving the kids to soccer, attending dance recitals, and helping with homework, I keep telling myself, *You're just not that old!*—because how can I be 50 when I'm living a life that 30 or 40 years ago belonged to women much younger than I am?

Maybe I don't feel 50 because people are living longer now, which means midlife comes later than it did for my parents. Today, midlife hits around age 40-43, not 35. So if I'm going to live until I'm 80-85, I'm not *that* much more than halfway there. But that doesn't mean my husband, David, and I are going to delay our retirement by 10 years. It means our retirement is going to stretch out 10 years longer than it used to. A friend of mine likes to say that 50 is the new 35. I love it! Here's the catch. In many ways it might be. And in many ways it's not. Retirement is not 30 years away. It's still 15.

Many of my friends, women my age, get so distracted with life in general that planning for retirement falls way to the bottom of their lists. We shove it to the back of our thoughts. It's not just my friends either. David's in his early fifties, yet he's still grappling with 40, and he swears he feels 29. He works like a dog, beats himself up at the gym (and pays for it later), and the other day, I caught him 30 feet up in one of our oak trees, thinning branches. Thirty feet! But even though David doesn't feel 50-something, he *is* planning for our retirement as though he's 50-something. It's *his* business to focus on retirement, on planning for all possibilities. Thank goodness.

I've seen David out there on the front lines, working with our sales team, putting together strategies for retirement that bring peace of mind. These strategies can eliminate the worry of not having enough to ever retire or out-living one's money in retirement. They gear these packages toward specific needs and incomes. They make it work. He's constantly telling me stories— hopeful stories, inspirational stories. These stories have motivated us to write this book to help you move forward. To devise a plan for the years ahead, so you can keep feeling vital, keep enjoying life. On your terms.

Here's the point. We don't feel our age, but we are our age, and one day, the years will catch up. I don't want anyone to wake up and suddenly find themselves 65, clutching their head, and thinking *Ahhhhhhhhhhhhhh! No retirement.* I don't want anyone to go through the agony and fear of sud-denly finding themselves looking at bleak years of counting their coins at the checkout stand. There's no need to.

I know boomers refuse to get old. We always have. We cut our teeth on being eternally youthful. But we're not. Time is going to catch up with each and every one of us, and we don't need to be unprepared. There are answers, and we have options, so take heart. And start planning now.

—NANCY ELLIS

THE AMERICAN RETIREMENT CRISIS

HOW MUCH TIME DO YOU SPEND getting ready for your vacation? We have seven kids, ranging from 5–23, and for our yearly vacation, we plan for months. We research vacation spots, buy plane tickets, reserve a car, book a hotel. We've got to pack for nine people. We set out seven sets of clothes for each person, one set for each day of our trip. Gather shoes, socks, pajamas, and medications. Band-Aids, Neosporin, hydrogen peroxide. Plan snacks and entertainment for the plane . . .

No matter whether you're one person or nine people, planning a vacation is a lot of work, and you have to put a lot of thought into it. We go away for a week, and we plan for a year before that. Our family has to budget and save to pay for that vacation. Why do we do it? Because we can see the reward at the end of the year. But here's the thing: did you know that most people spend more time planning and budgeting for a one-week vacation than they do planning for their retirement, which is a vacation that could last for more than 20 years? More than 20 years! We need to open our eyes and start doing some long-term planning because our retirement "vacations" aren't the same as they were in our parents' day.

We're facing a huge retirement crisis in the United States. Huge. In 2014, the last of the baby boomers turned 50. Between 1946 and 1964, 75,858,000 babies were born.[1] Every day from now until 2029, 10,000 of those boomers will turn 65. Think about it. Without adequate planning, how realistic is it that the baby boomers will all be able to retire at 65?

In the 2014 *Retirement Confidence Survey*,[2] polling workers aged 55 and older, 60 percent indicated they had less than $100,000 in savings and assets other than their homes, yet nearly two-thirds of those surveyed said they believed they were doing a pretty good job of preparing for retirement. And only 44 percent reported they and/or their spouses have tried to calculate how much money they will need to have saved by the time they retire so they can live comfortably in retirement. While each person's retirement needs are different, some financial advisors suggest $1 million per person and $2 million per couple. Something's off.

Why aren't more people planning for retirement? It's not too late. Map out what income you'll need in your retirement years, then talk with your financial advisor to create a retirement plan to finance your own retirement lifestyle.

Total Savings and Investments Reported by Workers

	2004	2009	2010	2011	2012	2013	2014
Less than $1,000		20%	27	29	30	28	36
$1,000 - $9,999	54%	19	16	17	18	18	16
$10,000 - $24,999		13%	11	10	12	11	8
$25,000 - $49,999	14%	11	12	11	10	9	9
$50,000 - $99,999	11%	12	11	9	10	10	9
$100,000 - $249,999	13%	12	11	14	11	12	11
$250,000 or more	9%	12	11	10	10	12	11

Source: Employee Benefit Research Institute and Greenwald & Associates,
2004–2014 Retirement Confidence Surveys

The Longest Vacation Ever

When you're creating your retirement plan, you need to factor in life expectancy. Maybe you think, as so many do, that you're not going to live that long, but life expectancy is rising. There's a huge difference between Americans' perception of their life expectancy and the reality. Did you know that 4 out of 10 people underestimate their life expectancy?[3] Why? Because the numbers change. As we age, our life expectancy actually increases. Each year we live means that we've survived all sorts of potential causes of death.

Life Expectancy of Males and Females in the United States

AGE	MALE LIFE EXPECTANCY	FEMALE LIFE EXPECTANCY
50	79.5	83.1
55	80.3	83.7
60	81.3	84.3
65	82.6	85.2
70	84.1	86.3
75	85.9	87.8
80	88.1	89.6
85	90.8	91.9

Source: Social Security Actuarial Life Table, 2010

When you turn 50, you'll probably live about another 30 years, until you're 80 years old. That's the equivalent of a 15-year vacation. If you make it to 65, you could live to be 85—a 20-year vacation. Of those who've reached age 65, 25 percent will live to be at least 90, and of those 25 percent, 10 percent will live to a ripe old age of 95 or more![4]

Probability of 65-year-old Living to Ages 80–100

AGE	MALE	FEMALE
80	60%	71%
85	40%	53%
90	20%	31%
95	6%	12%
100	1%	3%

Source: Social Security Actuarial Life Table, 2010

Underestimation of life expectancy increases the chances that retirees and pre-retirees will exhaust all their financial resources other than Social Security. This factor combined with a lack of retirement planning can result in inadequate funds for retirement.

Retirement Has Changed

Retirement planning has changed over the past 50 years. In our parents' day, retirement planners talked about the three-legged stool of retirement income: Social Security, traditional company pensions, and personal savings. Social Security provided a basic level of support that people supplemented with their pensions and personal savings. *So in our parents' day, the bulk of a retirement plan was pension, then savings, then Social Security.* But now, all that's changed. That stool now has two very wobbly legs—pensions and Social Security.

Traditional pensions are being replaced by plans such as 401(k)s and 403(b)s, where you, rather than your employer, contribute to your own retirement. With 401(k)s, companies often match your contribution up to a certain percentage, commonly six percent. With 403(b)s, matching contributions are

The Three-Legged Stool of Retirement

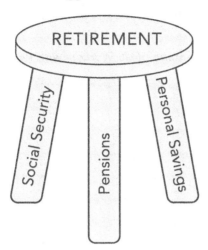

rare. As for Social Security benefits, they won't go away, but they'll most likely be less than the benefits our parents and grandparents enjoyed.

For boomers, savings and money put in retirement plans have become the primary focus, and though that leg is not as wobbly as pensions and Social Security, it's pretty shaky. The takeaway? Baby boomers are the first generation since the Great Depression without the safety net of pensions and other benefits their parents enjoyed.

Pensions Are Nearly Extinct

The days of life-long devotion to one company, send-off dinners, and a gold watch at retirement are long gone. So are pensions that helped to guarantee a carefree retirement. Today people skip from job to job, and employers have replaced pension plans with 403(b)s and matching 401(k)s. In 1979, 28 percent of all workers were enrolled in defined benefit plans (pension plans). By 2012, that number had dropped to 3 percent![5] It makes sense for corporations. With traditional pensions, the employer took all the investment risks. But with the stock market crash during 2000–2002, and along with increased government regulations, many employers began closing off traditional pension plans and offering contribution plans instead, where the employee takes the investment risk.[6]

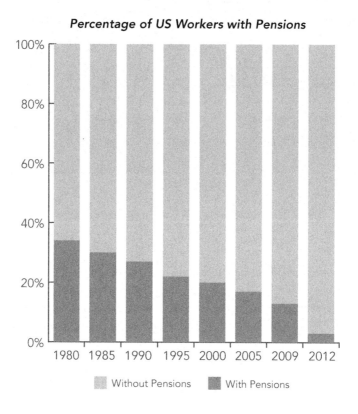

Percentage of US Workers with Pensions

There's more. Corporations are looking for ways to reduce expenses and create "leaner" companies, so they're reducing or eliminating their matching contributions. As a result of the 2007 financial crisis, 18 percent of 334 corporations surveyed suspended or reduced 401(k) contributions to conserve cash.[7] When the crisis eased, 23 percent of the companies that reinstated company matches offered less generous contributions than before the Great Recession of 2007.

Some companies, especially small businesses, offer no match at all. Since the lowest point of the Great Recession of 2007, the number of companies that match employee contributions to 401(k) plans has decreased by almost

7 percent, according to the 401(k) Performance Survey, conducted by American Investment Planners LLC in Jericho, NY.[8] Some companies have also cut expenses by delaying 401(k) matches until the end of the year or early the following year. In 2013, IBM followed this trend, offering a lump-sum payment, and paying at the beginning of the following year. Workers who left the company before December 15th didn't get their match for the year. You'll want to check out your company's retirement plans very carefully, and decide if that's the best place for you to put your money.

Social Security Is Running on Empty

Current predictions indicate that the Social Security trust fund will run out by 2037 if nothing is done. Without funding from another source, after 2037, retirees can pretty much expect to receive about 77 cents on every dollar of their scheduled benefits.[9] And retirement keeps getting pushed out. By 2027, the full retirement age will have completed its change from 65 to 67 years of age. And there are those who are advocating raising the age to 70 to help with shortfalls in the program. Social Security is too important to go away, but payroll taxes are likely to be greater in the future than they are now, and workers will probably have to work longer to receive full Social Security benefits. Yet more and more people are relying on Social Security for a greater percentage of their retirement. You don't have to. Talk to a financial advisor to explore how you can create a more balanced retirement plan. You *do* have options. In the next chapter, we'll discuss where you can find more money to set aside for your retirement vacation.

Savings Are Down

Boomers' parents lived with the post-war idea that anything was possible—owning their own home, two cars, and a color TV. They bought, but their sensibilities were still tinged by the Great Depression. On the other hand, their kids, boomers, also grew up with the idea that anything was possible, but without the shadow of the Great Depression. As credit became easy, they went wild—turning over their cars more often, buying more expensive homes, adding second floors to the homes they already owned, traveling, and sending kids to private schools.

When the Great Recession hit in 2007, they were forced to change their habits dramatically, possibly permanently. During the Great Recession of 2007, boomers lost 28 percent of their retirement savings, largely due to the sharp collapse in the stock market and home equity. As a result, 50 percent of boomers indicate they are delaying retirement, and 25 percent have come out of retirement and gone back to work to pay bills and to stretch their remaining retirement funds.[10] Even with their reduced spending, boomers need to focus on their own ability to save and prepare, instead of relying on others and hoping for the best—particularly at a time when life expectancy and medical costs are expected to continue to rise.

Working Indefinitely Is Not a Plan

When Nancy's mom was in her late forties, she and Nancy's dad divorced. She received little alimony but was incredibly resilient, working as a bookkeeper and raising six kids, which was overwhelming. She worked after they were grown, and planned on working until she was eligible for Social Security. After Nancy's mom started collecting Social Security, her plan—which was not really a plan—was to keep working as long as she could. But about eight years after the divorce, Nancy's younger brother, who was 31, passed away, and his death, in the wake of her divorce, sent Nancy's mom spiraling. She couldn't get over it. On top of that, her health went downhill. She'd had diabetes since her thirties, which she was keeping under control, but then she started having little strokes, and eventually had to stop working, at least 10 years before she'd planned to, with the resulting cut in benefits.

For a while Nancy's mom lived in an apartment, which wasn't a good situation. She was physically capable of being on her own, but her children worried that if she had a stroke or went into insulin shock, nobody would be there to help her. Plus she was lonely and sank even deeper into depression. She barely left the house, and when she did, it was often to go to the hospital. She was constantly in the hospital.

So the kids decided to put their mom in an assisted living program. She had no pension, no long-term care insurance, and her Social Security was only $900 per month. Nancy and her siblings needed to come up with the money. Well, any time there's money involved with a parent—whether they're giving it to you or you're giving it to them—things can get tense. It's a huge stress on the family. Nancy and her siblings started fighting, because nobody felt they had money to take care of their mom. They all felt awful—their mom was sick, and everyone was fighting. Imagine how Nancy's mom felt. She couldn't take care of herself. She had to ask her kids for help, and then her family was torn because of it.

Finally, Nancy and her brother, the two oldest kids, had to step up. It's been really tough. Since 2012, they've each paid $1,700 per month—a total of $3,400 per month or $40,800 per year. With medication distribution ($600 total each month), it's about $48,000 per year. It's humiliating for Nancy's mom to take money from her kids—not only the money they spend on her care, but she also has to ask for spending money sometimes. For example, she wants to buy gifts for her grandkids, but she can't afford it, so Nancy and her brother buy them for her. It makes her feel terrible, because she feels like we already do too much for her. She's always saying, "Oh, I'm a burden. I don't want to be a burden." It's a hardship on our families too. That's money that could be set aside for our own retirement.

But she's their mom. Of course they want to help her, and they're so grateful they can. She's happy there. She's extremely social and loves to chat, so they've made her an ambassador. She shows anyone new around—"This is our cafeteria. This is our theatre."—which boosts her self-worth. In her retirement, she's back to where she was years ago. Outgoing, on her game, involved. How could Nancy and her brother deny her that?

And think about this. She's single, and if she hadn't had Nancy and her brother, where would she be? What if you're single and don't have kids? Or you're putting such a huge burden on your kids that they might end up in the same boat? Things happen. Divorce, health issues. If Nancy's mom planned for those bumps, she'd be in much better shape, and so would her kids. But she didn't plan. And she regrets it every day of her life.

As Nancy's mom found, there are a lot of risks to relying on working longer, indefinitely, or even forever, as your retirement plan. Still, with a lack of savings, pensions all but obliterated, and more people relying on a shaky Social Security system for the bulk of their income, many retirees are thinking about going back to work, delaying retirement, or doing away with the idea of retirement altogether.

Going Back to Work

During the Great Recession of 2007 and in the years following, millions of older workers were downsized or out of employment. Millions wanted to work, but they couldn't find jobs. Data shows that only 31 percent of those older workers aged 55 to 64 who were displaced between 2007 and 2009 regained full-time employment by 2010.[11] Rather than keep up the humiliating hunt, or take work that paid significantly less, they retired. In fact, a 2013 MetLife study indicated that 25 percent said they did so earlier than planned due to loss of job or job opportunities.[12]

Those lucky enough to find a job often land employment that pays very little, and employers cut hours to fewer than 20 to avoid paying benefits. Even that work isn't very easy to come by. Older workers are competing with a huge, much younger—and less expensive—population.

Delaying Retirement

The Great Recession of 2007 pushed back the planned date of retirement for two-fifths of pre-retirees from age 45 and up. A 2013 survey showed that 15 percent of those polled who had retired since 2008 retired earlier than planned because of the recession.

Among those ages 55–64 who had not yet retired:

- 18 percent planned to follow the traditional retirement model of working full-time until a set date and then stop working altogether.

- 24 percent expected to keep working as long as possible.

- 18 percent expected to retire and then work a part-time job.

- 9 percent expected to retire and then become self-employed.[13]

We know people who have worked until 70 or into their early 70s. They were able to put off dipping into their savings. The money they saved combined with the money they earned has made a huge difference in their lifestyle for when they finally did retire. It's a possibility. If you own your own business, you might be in good shape. Depending on your business, you can probably pretty much set your retirement age. If you work for a company, and can stay until your late 60s, that's great. Here's the thing, though: With the dramatic rise of age discrimination claims, some of us might not have that option.[14]

Putting off Retirement Altogether

Imagine how much more difficult it may be if you hope to avoid retirement altogether. If you do have a job, how long can you realistically hold on to it? You have to at least consider the possibility of failing health. What happens if your health fails and you're left unprepared? If you don't consider that possibility, then what?

Working Yourself into the Ground

On the other end of the spectrum, say you can find the work, but you're so panicked about your retirement and the fact that at some point you won't work that you worry constantly and work until you drop. The thought of retirement can be especially frightening if you're single and don't have any kids. Take David's sister. She's 60, and she's so worried about being 82 without enough money that she works all the time—partly to get by and partly to save. She works for Parks and Recreation five days a week, and she waits tables on the weekend, where she works from six o'clock in the morning until three o'clock in the afternoon. She's one person who does not save any money to go on vacation. She saves it to retire.

She has a car and a condo. She has a decent job. She's saving. She has about $100,000 in savings, but even with that, she's consumed with worry that she can never stop working, can never retire, because she won't have enough money. Finally, David sat down with her and talked her through it. She's not quite where she wants to be, but she's in much better shape than she previously thought.

As David showed his sister, you can make a plan. She still has time, but she definitely needs to start planning to make her goals. Don't put it off until it's too late. Enjoying life is wonderful, but there's a happy medium. And look at David's sister. If you put together a plan, you'll be surprised at how much easier it is to create an income stream during retirement. That way, you can relax and enjoy the time before you do retire, with the peace of mind that you'll have a sufficient income during retirement. You don't want to spend every waking moment doing everything you can, working round the clock, and still worrying. So follow David's sister's lead, and seek financial advice.

The first step is to take a breath. The situation might not look rosy, but think about this: At the end of the day, if you live in the United States, you have a roof over your head, and food to eat, you're in better shape than most of the people in the world. Read on, and we'll help you get to a brighter, more secure retirement future.

KEY POINTS

- **People spend more time planning a one-week vacation than planning their retirement. Have you done your due diligence? Work with a financial advisor to develop a retirement plan.**

- **The three-legged retirement stool is wobbling. Social Security is still intact but benefits may be reduced. Pensions are nearly obsolete. 401(k)s are going away. So it's time to start thinking of new ways to create a monthly income. There are ways.**

- **Planning to keep working is not a plan—the job market is tough, and you can't guarantee your health.**

- **There's hope! It's possible. Read on.**

HOW TO FIND THE MONEY

WHEN NANCY AND I STARTED to make our transition into the life insurance business, I recruited a seasoned agent named John Carlile, with whom I worked in the health insurance market for years. He was one of my many mentors and was at least twenty years my senior—gray hair, extremely wise, with years of experience. I provided him with the leads, and he went on the sales calls. People trusted John, because he came from a place of integrity, was incredibly knowledgeable about life insurance, and had a way of cutting to the heart of the matter. I sometimes felt because of John's age and experience, he got away with being direct in a way that I didn't feel I could. At the time, I lacked both gray hair and his many, many years of experience in the insurance marketplace.

I would get frustrated when I couldn't convince families they needed protection to secure their future, especially when their families were completed unprotected. I wanted to help them, but I didn't know how to get through to them like John could. Yet I always rallied, and went back to work the next day more driven and determined.

John shared with me the story of two prospective clients, a young couple in their thirties with two young kids and no life insurance. While the kids watched TV in the family room, John sat at the kitchen table with the couple. He said the wife asked questions about college, paying off debts, wanting to double up on mortgage payments, savings, concerns she had, priorities about where to spend their money. John thought he could really help this couple, but just as they were starting to pin down the details, including cost, the couple exchanged a glance. With one glance, an entire conversation took place—they couldn't afford it yet.

"We both work," the wife said. "If something happened to one of us, we would still have one salary. We'd get by."

John said he simply took a breath, paused, then asked, "If you don't mind my asking, are your kids watching cable TV?"

The couple nodded.

"How much does cable TV cost you monthly?" John asked. "Sixty, eighty dollars?"

"About that," the wife replied.

John then scratched his head—it's a way he had that, not intentionally, fooled people into thinking he was slightly confused—and said, "So think about it. You're saying that your kids watching television is more import-ant to you than writing a sixty dollar monthly check that would pay off this home, so your kids would have a place to stay if you were hit by a car tomorrow, and so they could also still go to college?"

John had given the couple something to think about. They discussed the insurance in more detail and purchased the policy.

As my mentor, John was always sharing stories that challenged me. But more importantly, he gave me the confidence to stop letting my age and lack of gray prevent me from finding a way to help and protect families by assisting them to find money, and at times to reallocate their spending and their priorities.

Americans waste a lot of money each year. Up to half a trillion dollars by some estimates. True, our spending habits are far more frugal than before the Great Recession of 2007—we're holding onto our cars longer, shopping at Target and Walmart. But there are some areas where we haven't cut back, areas we might not even think about. Areas where we could "find money" to put toward securing our future. With far less per month than you might imagine, you can greatly increase your retirement security. In this chapter, we'll show you areas to save money on entertainment, food, traffic tickets, energy, credit cards and ATM fees, and more.

Entertainment

In 2012, the average household spent approximately $2,600 on entertainment. This figure included nearly $1,000 for audio and visual equipment and services, more than $600 for media fees and admissions, and nearly $650 for toys, hobbies, and pets.[1] And don't get us going on dieting. Marketdata Enterprises estimated that the weight-loss market would hit $66 billion in 2013. No, your eyes aren't deceiving you. According to them, there are 108 million American dieters and they make 4 to 5 dieting attempts per year.[2]

In 2013, revenues from the sale of video games alone in the United States reached $17.4 billion.[3] Premium cable packages, which include phone, Internet, and cable, can be expensive—these plans can cost more than $100 per month. An HBO subscription alone can cost upwards of $10 per month.[4] Dropping cable, satellite, or other pay TV services while still getting your entertainment fix takes a bit more effort. However, you can find all kinds of guides outlining ways to watch shows and movies via the Internet or streaming services like Netflix. Cutting your cable and some home entertainment can save you an average of about $75 a month.[5] That's $900 a year.

Food and Beverages

We all know about using Groupon, looking for bargains, shopping sales, and taking advantage of coupon books when eating out. Here are just a few statistics to give you some perspective. We spend $165 billion on wasted food each year.[6] That's food that we leave on our plates and scrape into the compost bin, or produce we forgot about or didn't get around to cooking. We're not just throwing out food, we're throwing away money—approximately $529 per person, per year.[7] To reduce this waste, try searching the Internet. There are a lot great sites out there that offer tips on how to not waste food.

Eating Out

In a recent survey, 58 percent of American adults reported they dine out at least once a week.[8] Here's the breakdown: 40 percent say they typically go out to a restaurant once a week, 14 percent go out two or three times a week, and 4 percent dine out more than three times a week. At an average cost of $15 per meal, you could be spending as much as $15 to $75 dollars per person per week, or $780 to $3,900 per year. The savings from eating just one of those meals at home adds up.

US Dining Expenses: At Home Versus Away from Home, 1960–2013

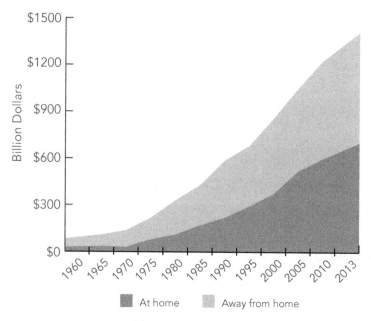

Source: USDA, Economic Research Service, Food Expenditure Series

Empty Calories

Do you love soda? Lots of people do. We spend $76 billion on soda each year.[9] We all know these drinks provide no nutritional value (or a negative value), and we're better off drinking water. Yet nearly half of Americans drink soda daily. If you think the soda intake is high, take a look at candy. In 2013, US confectionery sales totaled an additional $33.6 billion.[10] That's $102 per person! Well, at least nearly 60 percent was for chocolate—that makes it better, right?

Coffee

According to a recent survey of American workers, folks who regularly buy coffee from designer coffee shops throughout the week spend, on average, $1,092 on coffee annually.[11] Each. Try making coffee at home and taking a thermos to work. Think of mochas as a splurge rather than a necessity.

Traffic Tickets

If you drive too fast or park in the wrong spot, you're throwing money at the government and raising your auto insurance premiums. Americans spend 6 billion dollars annually on speeding tickets alone, which translates into 41 million tickets at an average ticket cost of approximately $150 each, and half of them can result in insurance penalties.[12] These penalties can cost approximately $300 annually. Take a deep breath, and remember that you're probably not saving more than a minute or two if you speed. Is it worth it?

Doctor Visits

With increasingly high health insurance deductibles, visits to the doctor are often out of pocket. Visiting an online certified doctor for many minor health concerns can often make sense. Call from your computer or a mobile app. You don't have to miss work or find a sitter for the kids, and the cost is much less than an unnecessary visit to your doctor.

Energy

In 2014, it was calculated that annual energy costs amounted to nearly $400 billion and that consumers could cut their energy expenses by one-third if they followed these recommendations from the government-backed Energy Star program.[13]

- Changing your air filter every three months at the minimum and using a programmable thermostat could save you over $180 a year.

- Lowering your water heat thermostat from 140 to 120 degrees can save you more than $400 a year.

- Americans waste $9 billion on energy-inefficient lighting. Replacing five light bulbs with Energy Star bulbs or fixtures can save you $70 per year.

- You could save $40 a year by using only cold water to wash your clothes, and as much as $36 per year by using the smallest pot necessary on your stove.

- In the average home, 75 percent of the electricity used to power home electronics and appliances is consumed while the products are turned off. Make sure to unplug your appliances when they might not be used for extended periods of time.

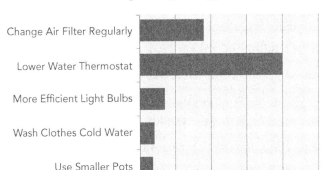

Annual Savings Using Energy Star Tips

Credit Card Interest

Currently, the average credit card debt per US household is $15,611. Americans owe a total of $882.6 billion in credit card debt.[14] A recent survey indicates that 21 percent carry more than $1,000 in debt from month-to-month and 15 percent of credit card households carry a month-to-month balance of over $2,500.[15] If you maintain a balance of $5,000 a month on a credit card with a 12 percent interest rate, you will spend $600 a year on interest. If you carry credit card debt, see if you can work with your credit card carrier to reduce payments or seek assistance from an advisor who specializes in this field. You'll need to pay for an advisor's services, but you'll save in the long run.

ATM Fees

We can't always avoid using an ATM from a bank other than our own. In 2011, the average fee for out-of-network ATM users was $3.81 per transaction. The annual total amount for ATM fees in 2010 was $7 billion.[16] If you find yourself running up major ATM charges, you might consider shifting your accounts to a credit union.

Gambling

We're not talking just about slot machines and 21 in Las Vegas casinos, which hit $11 billion in 2014.[17] We're talking about fantasy football, which *Forbes Magazine* estimated at $15 billion in 2012, based on reports from the Fantasy Sports Trade Association.[18] And we're talking about lottery tickets, which took in over $68 billion in 2013.[19] In fact, since their inception in 1965, lottery ticket sales have increased every single year. *The Huffington Post* claims a person's chance of winning the lottery on a single ticket is one in 175 million. You're more likely to be struck by lightning (1 in 3,000)[20] or killed by a shark (1 in 3.7 million).[21] Think about it.

KEY POINTS

- Take stock of where you spend money, and where you can cut back. With a little ingenuity and perseverance, you'd be surprised where you could find money.

- Make a plan to get out of debt and stay debt-free. Then stick to your plan.

- It can take very little per month to allocate your money to a plan to help secure your future. Determine what amount you can spend each month, and consistently put that money toward retirement. Sure, the amount of your savings is important, but even more important is consistency.

THE AMERICAN DREAM—OWNING YOUR OWN HOME

ONE OF OUR TEAM MEMBERS contributed this story about a woman debating whether or not to buy a new home. A few years ago, when she and her husband divorced, she took some of her share of the sale of the house, which at that time wasn't huge, bought a condo, and worked like crazy to pay it off in five years, before she hit 55. Last year, she met the love of her life. They're getting married. Her place is too small for both of them, and they want to buy a house together. She's built some equity in her current home. He rents and has no equity. She has some retirement, but not enough. They plan on working, well, forever. They're both self-employed, so as long as they're in good health, they have a better chance of determining their retirement date than if they worked for someone else.

The two of them would like a house large enough for her two kids (mid-twenties) to visit with (hopefully someday) her grandkids. They also want space to entertain. He wants a big yard, which is a lot of work, plus at some point, as he gets older, he might need help. On the other hand, she doesn't want a yard. She's opting out of maintenance—that's on him. They like the idea of a 15-year mortgage, but without knowing exactly what their income will be over the next few years, they're thinking of going for a 30-year mortgage, and paying extra when they can. They have to live someplace. They want to live someplace they love. They also want to travel, a lot.

She's looking at all of her options: Sell her condo, put her profits toward retirement, and rent? Sell her condo, buy a smaller house instead of a larger home and yard, and allocate a portion of what she saves each month to a retirement fund? Buy a house, then sell it if they need to (when it's anyone's guess what the market will be)? Buy a house, and if they need to, look into a reverse mortgage, so they can borrow against the house, live there until they die, and possibly have nothing left for their loved ones? She also really wants to leave money to her kids. So what's the best way to protect her assets and put her money to work for her? It's a lot to think about.

To Buy or Not to Buy

For many people, owning a home is the fulfillment of the American dream, but when you reach your pre-retirement and retirement years, you might want to re-examine that dream and weigh your options for the years ahead. Maybe you've paid off your mortgage, or you're doubling up payments to pay off your mortgage before you retire. Maybe you're thinking about buying a new place altogether—downsizing, possibly moving into a gated community with common grounds, where you'll enjoy a close neighborhood and the benefits of trees and a lawn without the hassle of maintenance. Or maybe you're considering buying a larger home to accommodate visiting children and grandchildren.

When you think about buying a home (at any age), or holding on to your home (at whatever cost), you're talking about a major financial move, so you're wise to look carefully at the pros and cons. Examine the positive and negative aspects of owning a home based on your personal desires, future plans, locale, and general financial situation.

Flexibility versus Settling In

If you tend to move around or frequently relocate for your job, renting a home has definite benefits. If you want to stay put, owning might be the answer for you.

Rent: Renting allows you to become acquainted with an area before making the longer-term commitment to own. Unless you're certain about a specific neighborhood, renting allows time for research and discovery. It's also easier to move. If you think you might need to move in the near future, whether it's because you are contemplating a job change or are planning to move to a different part of the county for retirement, you might want to rent. Buying ties you down to a greater extent.

Own: Once you commit to owning a home, you're more likely to become involved in your community, because you know you'll likely be there for years. You can get to know your neighbors, join a home-owners association, or volunteer for projects that benefit the community. However, your home is not a liquid asset. That means that it's hard to quickly convert to cash. If you need to sell your home because of a change in your circumstances, you may not be able to as quickly as you'd like or for as much money as you want.

Maintenance and Utilities

When deciding whether to rent or own, make sure to consider the additional costs of maintaining your home.

Rent: In many instances, your landlord will pay for utilities such as water, sewer, garbage, and, in some cases, even heat. When a pipe leaks, you don't head to the store—you pick up the phone and call the landlord.

Own: As a homeowner, you must spend time and money keeping your home in good repair—your roof, painting inside and out, maintaining carpet or wood floors. Plus, you need to set aside funds for unexpected expenses, such as flooding, a new hot water heater, or the need to replace leaking windows.

Tax Advantages

Seems like a no-brainer, right? You rent, you don't pay property taxes. But there are also advantages to paying that tax.

Rent: The advantage is that you don't pay property taxes. However, you don't get a tax advantage from renting.

Own: You can deduct mortgage interest and your property taxes from your federal income tax calculations. In addition, those who work from home may be eligible to take deductions for their home office and portions of utilities. If you sell your home and meet certain requirements, you gain additional tax benefits. The IRS won't apply a "capital gains" tax on your profits from the sale of your home. If you're single, you can keep the first $250,000 in profit you make when selling the home. If you're married, you can keep the first $500,000 in profit.

Monthly Payments and Equity

There are financial benefits and opportunities to grow your assets for each scenario. You want to decide which works best for you.

Rent: When you pay rent, you're helping pay your landlord's mortgage or adding to his or her bank account, not yours. Rents have been rising in many cities, so when your current lease ends, your monthly housing payment is likely to increase. Your rent is a big-budget item that can change often, so long-term budgeting can be tough. On the other hand, you have extra money to put toward a potential nest egg or income stream (annuity) because your rent will probably be lower than a mortgage payment, and if the rent climbs or your income decreases, you can move.

Own: Home ownership requires you to have a stable or growing income because you have committed to a long-term loan with a substantial monthly payment. However, when you have a home mortgage, you increase your degree of ownership in your home with every payment by building equity. A general rule is that if you intend to stay in your property for at least five to seven years, the costs of purchasing the home are more likely to be offset by how much you've put in (accrued equity) plus the increased housing value.

Creative Control

You'll also want to consider how important it is that you have creative control over how your home looks and that it reflects your aesthetic tastes.

Rent: Some landlords may let you paint your apartment, but you'll have to get their permission and consult on the color. And you'll probably need to pay to have it returned to the original color when you leave. More likely than not, you won't be able to change the carpet. You can often negotiate window treatments. You just need to determine how important creative control is to you.

Own: One of the joys of homeownership is that you can change your environment to suit your tastes. You can remodel, you can add on. Before each change, you want to weigh how much of the money you've put into your home you'll get back if or when you sell, how important the updates are to you, and how you might put that money to work in other ways.

OWNING VERSUS RENTING: PROS AND CONS

	OWN	RENT
Flexibility or Settling In	You're more likely to become involved in your community.	Allows you to become acquainted with an area before making the longer-term commitment to own.
Maintenance & Utilities	You're on the hook for all home expenditures, including emergencies.	Your landlord may pay for utilities such as water, sewer, and garbage, and he or she is responsible for maintenance and emergencies.
Tax Advantages	You can deduct mortgage interest and your property taxes from your federal income tax calculations.	You don't pay property taxes, but you don't get tax advantages.
Monthly Payments & Equity	You increase your degree of ownership in your home with every payment by building equity.	You're helping to increase your landlord's equity—it's their investment, not yours.
Creative Control	You can remodel, add on—change your environment to suit your needs and tastes.	You may be able to change the paint color, but that's probably the extent of the changes you can make.

Determine What's Right for You

You'll want to take a long look at the advantages and disadvantages of owning your home versus renting. There's really no right or wrong answer. In the long run, it depends on what works for you.

Can a Reverse Mortgage Help Fund My Retirement?

One of the products gaining in popularity in recent years is the reverse mortgage, which is being used as retirees look for ways to improve their cash flow. A reverse mortgage allows homeowners to borrow against their home equity, while still maintaining ownership of the home. We've all seen the commercials—some handsome, older, male, media idol telling us about how these vehicles can help make our retirement years wonderful. And maybe they can. And maybe they can't. A reverse mortgage can be a valuable retirement planning tool that can greatly increase your retirement income streams by letting you use your largest asset—your home. But, as with any big financial decision, it has its advantages and disadvantages, so it's important to do careful research and consult a reputable advisor before jumping off the cliff.

What Is a Reverse Mortgage?

A reverse mortgage is a type of home equity loan that allows you to borrow against the equity, while still maintaining ownership of the home. However, unlike "regular" home equity loans, a reverse mortgage doesn't require that you have income or particularly good credit—it's all about the equity in your home. If you're at least 62 years of age and considering a reverse mortgage, several factors determine how much you can borrow. Most important are the values of your home, your age, and interest rates.

Here's how it works. You receive the money from the loan—you can choose lump sum, regular installments, or line of credit—but you don't have to make payments on it. Instead, the lenders collect when you sell the house, permanently move out of your home—possibly to an assisted living community, or you die. In most cases, the proceeds from the sale of your home are used to make the repayment.

What Are the Benefits of a Reverse Mortgage?

A reverse mortgage can be a powerful source of funding for individuals who need to increase their income to be comfortable in retirement. The largest personal asset most retirees possess is their home, and in many cases, it's paid off or pretty close to it. A reverse mortgage can increase income without increasing monthly payments and allow a retiree to stay in his or her home.

Tax-Free Money

Honestly, how many times in your life do you have a shot at tax-free money? It seems that no matter where you get your money from, the government always has a way of getting its share. In the case of a reverse mortgage, however, that isn't necessarily true. Most reverse mortgage income is tax-free, because it is classified as a loan. That means that you can receive every penny of the loan and not lose a percentage of it to the government.

Fewer Restrictions

Many loans come with a tight set of restrictions as to what can be done with the money. For example, a car loan can only be used for the purchase of a car. However, the money you receive from a reverse mortgage has no strings attached. Often people use this additional revenue to live the life they've dreamed of. You can pay for vacations, recreational activities, and more. And no more monthly mortgage payments!

Safety and Security

Since the most popular of all reverse mortgages, the Home Equity Conversion Mortgage (or HECM), is managed and backed by the federal government, you don't have to be concerned about your lender defaulting. This can really reduce the stress involved with making this big decision. Thanks to the involvement of the federal government in this program, you can rest easy knowing the reverse mortgage will play out exactly as you expect.

An Easier Transaction

If you have purchased a home in the past, you know how difficult the traditional mortgage process can be. There is a ton of paperwork, credit checks, and other various factors that determine what kind of loan you qualify for. With a reverse mortgage, the process is much easier on you. It's just based on the value of the home, your age, and interest rates. There is no income qualification required to take out a reverse mortgage, so your personal finances will not be cross-examined as they are when taking out a normal mortgage.

What about the Downside?

Among the negatives of a reverse mortgage are the costs involved. Many people who take reverse mortgages have no idea of the costs because the terms can be so complex and difficult to understand. All mortgages have costs, but reverse mortgage fees, which can include the interest rate, loan origination fee, mortgage insurance fee, appraisal fee, title insurance fees, and various other closing costs, are extremely high when compared with a traditional mortgage.

You Might Need Nursing Home Care in the Future

If you take on the debt of a reverse mortgage, you're okay as long as you can live in that home. If you have to move out of the home into assisted living or a nursing home, the mortgage becomes due. There you are, having to pay off the loan while also paying the high cost of assisted living or nursing home care. Here's a grim scenario: You borrow, say, $200,000 and end up needing care 24/7—that reverse mortgage cash will be exhausted in about two years or less. Then what? If you are not prepared for this situation, you can end up in a Medicaid-paid nursing home or dependent on the kindness of others.

You Might Want to Move

Do you think you might want to move out of your home someday? How about a warmer climate? Since you'll have to pay off the loan balance when you move out for more than 12 consecutive months, you might end up feeling stuck in a place you no longer want to be.

Any Dependent Living in the Home Is Affected

These days, it's all too common for a child or even their families to move back home because of financial hardship. If you have a reverse mortgage and you need to go into an assisted living facility, they have to find another place to live. They're considered tenants, and according to the rules of the reverse mortgage, they have to leave when you do. Imagine telling a child that they're being kicked out of their home.

Even without a Mortgage Payment, There's Still the Possibility of Default

If you have a reverse mortgage, run low on cash, and fail to pay property taxes or keep up the property insurance on the home, you are in default and a lender can then foreclose. Even failing to maintain the property can trigger a default. If you do default, your lender is in a good position to take over the property and then flip it for a good profit.

When You Die, Your Beneficiaries Must Pay Off the Loan

The entire principal, plus accrued interest and service fees, must be paid in full to the lender before beneficiaries can legally take possession of the home. If property values have decreased, this debt may exceed the actual market value of the home. If they can't pay the debt, the lender has the right to foreclose and sell the property. At best, the reverse mortgage will almost always decrease the equity in your home, which will leave less money to your beneficiaries.

One Example

There are many stories about times when a reverse mortgage isn't necessarily the right choice to make. One such story is about a woman who owned her home outright and lived on her Social Security, a small payment from her 401(k), and income from her part-time job, working for a local accountant. With this income, she was able to make ends meet plus take the occasional weekend away with her girlfriends, and spoil her grandsons now and then.

One day, after visiting the doctor, she discovered she had cancer. With treatment and an excellent prognosis, she continued to work for the accountant. Despite her prognosis, her illness progressed and, exhausted from more aggressive chemotherapy, she had to quit her job. For the first time since her early twenties, she juggled bills, called the electric company for an occasional extension, and counted every item she put in her shopping cart.

Then she read an article about reverse mortgages. She signed the papers and felt as though a huge weight had been lifted from her shoulders. Her daughter was more reserved, pressing her mom for details about how the loan worked. Her mom was vague—the terms were complex—but she was clear about one detail: she now had an additional income of $2,000 a month for 10 years. She could breathe when bills came due. She was still responsible for paying property taxes and insurance, and for all maintenance, but with the extra income, she felt she'd be okay. After 10 years, if she lived that long, she'd be allowed to stay in the house that now belonged to the lenders, but she'd receive no more income, and she'd still be responsible for taxes and maintenance.

Fifteen months later, knocked flat on her back from a cold on top of chemo, she failed to pay her property insurance, the loan company foreclosed, and she was without an income and a place to live. She stayed with her daughter for the last few months of her life. While she did receive initial benefits from her loan, it didn't pay off.

Each story is different, of course. Just know that taking out a reverse mortgage is not a decision to be taken lightly.

KEY POINTS

- Homeownership is not for everyone. Consider your financial situation, lifestyle, future plans, and desire.

- Reverse mortgages can help provide security after retirement, but they often come with a price. Before signing on the dotted line, weigh all your options and check with your advisor.

DIGGING
OUT OF DEBT

BABY BOOMERS ARE BEING CALLED the Debt Generation. There's a good reason for it. As we noted before, the problem is partially because they're a product of their parents' generation, the Greatest Generation. After World War II, the world was open to them—new home, washer and dryer, two cars, and a color TV in a maple console—all on monthly payment plans. Those who could, spent like crazy, but even then, the shadow of the Great Depression helped them keep their spending in check.

Having no mental-check system of memories of horribly lean years, boomers whipped out their credit cards for everything from groceries to new bathrooms to private schools, without worrying about how they would later pay the debt. During these flush years, home equity became their personal piggy banks until the Great Recession of 2007 hit, causing real estate to tank and stocks to dive. Despite the recession, the cost of education continued to rise, resulting in an overall increase of 1,120 percent since 1978—higher than consumer goods, food, shelter, and medical care.[1] The increased cost of education in turn led to larger loans being taken out and an increased number of student loans. Many boomers were forced to use their credit cards to make ends meet, and many, trying to crawl out of debt and recover from depleted savings, have been forced to rethink retirement strategies, such as delaying retirement, semi-retiring by getting a part-time job, or never retiring at all, which are solutions, true, but not failsafe.

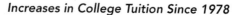

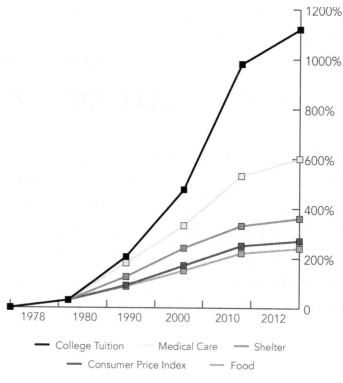

Increases in College Tuition Since 1978

Bloomberg and Bureau of Labor Statistics

Boomer Debt at a Glance

Millions of Americans age 65 and older are in debt from unpaid student loans. They owed about $18.2 billion in 2013, which is up from just $1.8 billion in 2005.[2] It's a catch-22—boomers keep working to pay for their millennial kids who can't find jobs, and in doing so, they hold onto jobs that could go to their millennial kids. It's the Great Depression all over again, when Franklin D. Roosevelt started Social Security, encouraging people to retire to make room in the workforce for the next generation. The difference is that Social Security only was meant to augment pension plans. This generation, however, doesn't have pensions to fall back on, so many have to continue working.

Then we have credit cards. Compared with the Greatest Generation, Generation X, and millennials, baby boomers have the highest average balance on credit cards ($5,347) and the highest average number of credit cards per person (2.66).[3]

Before the Great Recession of 2007, conventional wisdom was to pay off your large debts prior to retirement. That way, retirement savings and portfolios would not be encumbered by large payments, such as mortgages, credit cards, car loans, or student loan debt.

Now, many US boomers are taking another route. Many are being forced to postpone retirement while they work to cover debt payments and fixed expenses that might not be covered by Social Security, pensions, and savings. Many more are struggling with the after-effects of credit card use, and are working with financial professionals to create a cash-management plan that they can stick to before leaving work.[4] And some, when faced with rising healthcare and education costs, depleted savings, and debt, have taken up the idea of letting their beneficiaries deal with the aftermath, and maintaining their debt to retain their current lifestyles.

In fact, according to a poll commissioned by Canadian bank CIBC, about one-quarter of retiring boomers surveyed expected to carry some debt into their retirement. More important, roughly 80 percent of those surveyed indicated that they had no plans to pay off their debt anytime soon and would stay in debt throughout their retirement.[5] While the study focused on Canadian participants, a similar trend is occurring here in the United States.[6]

Student Loan Debt

During the Great Recession of 2007, a single mom with two kids—14 and 16—was laid off from her job as an IT professional. The company she worked for said the layoff was due to general cutbacks and a new "lean" policy, but she couldn't shake the feeling that ageism had something to do with it.

She sent out dozens of resumes and sat on the edge of her seat through one grueling interview after another, but she couldn't get in the door. Her track record was excellent, her references impeccable, but she couldn't catch a break.

Finally, she started working as a freelance contractor and went back to school to brush up on her degree and take business classes so she could open her own IT consulting business, which would allow her to work pretty much as long as she wanted. Although the road was tough, looking back, she's actually grateful for losing her job, which caused her to make the change. She loves her work, and her new business is doing really well.

But in addition to taking out student loans, which she's now paying off, she dipped heavily into her savings. And now her kids are getting closer to college. Even with her kids taking out loans, which they'll have to do, she'll need to co-sign for those loans, and if her kids don't find jobs right away—which is the case with many of her friends' kids—she'll be liable for those bills. On top of it all, retirement is out there. Somewhere. So on top of paying off her student loans, she needs to rebuild her retirement. She's in a bind, because she's taken on new liabilities when she should be saving for retirement, and she's sacrificing her lifestyle now and after retirement because of it. As long as she can work, she'll be okay, but how realistic is it that she'll be able to work forever?

Many older Americans are shouldering greater student loan balances, whether from their education or their kids' education. Student debt is the only kind of household debt that continued to rise throughout the Great Recession of 2007. Totaling nearly $1 trillion, it now has the second largest balance after mortgage debt, with a 70 percent increase in both the number of borrowers, and in average balance per person between 2004 and 2012.[7] In fact, many have taken out a home equity line of credit (HELOC) to finance tuition.

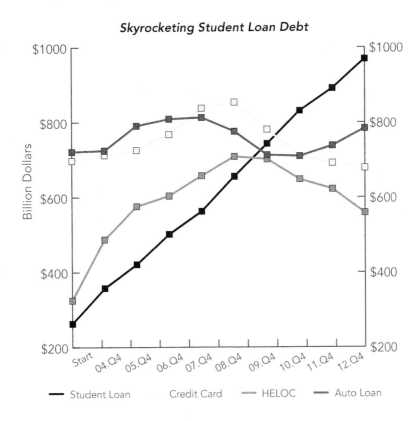

Skyrocketing Student Loan Debt

Legend: — Student Loan   Credit Card   — HELOC   — Auto Loan

In addition to the disproportionate rise in education costs, reasons for astronomical student loan balances include: a greater number of students in general, including adults returning to school, increased need for financial assistance, students staying longer in college, more students attending graduate school, and the balance of the debt staying with the borrower.

More students. More people are attending college and graduate school despite the skyrocketing tuition and fees. Why? Statistics still prove that higher education leads to greater overall lifetime earnings, and more companies are requiring higher degrees even for entry-level positions.

Increased need for financial assistance. Because of skyrocketing tuition, more students are in need of loans but they are too young to get credit, so parents are taking out student loans for their children.

Students are staying longer in college and more often attend graduate school. Because of the financial crisis in higher education, colleges must frequently offer a reduced number of required courses per semester. This in turn makes it difficult for students to sign up for the courses they need to graduate, so they need to stay in school longer. Also, because of the rising costs of tuition, an increasing number of students are working part-time to keep down the cost of their loans. As a result, it's difficult for them to maintain a full course load.[8] In fact, according to the Education Trust, a nonprofit agency based in Washington DC, 60 percent of those earning a bachelor's degree take six years to do so. In addition to the difficulties getting into required classes, millennials are going on to graduate school as a way to buffer themselves from the real world, hoping that the job market will be more favorable by the time they graduate.

In many cases the balance stays with the borrower. Student loans, like back taxes, don't go away. If you file Chapter 7 or Chapter 13 bankruptcy, you may not need to repay your loan, but only if the bankruptcy court finds that repayment would impose undue hardship on you and your dependents. The decision is made in an adversary proceeding in bankruptcy court, meaning you're on the defensive and your creditor can attack and argue against you.

As a result of the increased need for student loans, and the high cost of those loans, pre-retirees and new retirees are sacrificing their current lifestyle and robbing their future retirement to help put their kids through school.

Credit Card Debt

One couple, both of whom are 55 years of age, are in a tough place now. Instead of saving to go on that long vacation known as retirement, they're digging their way out of nearly $18,000 in credit card debt.

Their debt pretty much snuck up on them—a tune-up here, a new computer there, helping their two boys with college and living expenses, a crown (and no dental insurance), so there's another $1,000 on the card. Their credit card payments are about $325 a month—spread across four cards, and that's just the minimum. They can barely keep up with the payments, let alone pay more each month, so the balance stays the same. They feel like it will stay the same forever.

In addition to their credit cards, they have two car payments and a mortgage. They don't want to saddle their kids with their debts. But this couple is resourceful—they're still working, they've cut back on their expenses, and they're working with David to develop a retirement plan. But I'm telling you, they never saw this coming.

Many Americans over 50 are struggling with a large amount of credit card debt. To help put it into perspective, a recent study showed that low- and middle-income households of older Americans who owed on a credit card for three months or more have racked up an average of $8,278 in debt.

These charges aren't for charging vacations, expensive watches, and new living room furniture. Half of the households 50 and older are using their credit cards for the basics—groceries, gas, and utilities. Fifty percent are also charging medical expenses such as prescription drugs. And no one in the study was paying off the credit they incurred every month.[9]

Lay Down Your Shovel and Stop Digging

So how do you get out of debt before retirement so you can enjoy your long vacation?

Dip into Your 401(k) to Pay Off Debt?

Dipping into your retirement savings to pay off credit card debt can seem like a good idea at first glance, but that's not necessarily true. We know that taking a 401(k) loan can seem like a great idea for a few reasons—you don't have to qualify, you can get the funds quite quickly, and the interest rate is typically about four to five percent, far below the typical credit card interest rate.

Most 401(k) plans allow you to borrow 50 percent of your balance, up to $50,000, which you have to pay back with interest through automatic payroll deductions. Typically, the loan must also be repaid within five years.

Nearly half of all retirement savers who have taken a 401(k) loan said they had borrowed the cash to pay down debt.[10] But dipping into these funds can be the single worst thing a pre-retiree can do to sabotage a retirement. There are a lot of things that can go wrong.

You're taking a chunk out of your current savings balance *and* you're missing out on higher compound returns those funds could have gained over time. Another thing, borrowing from your 401(k) isn't free. You'll pay the loan back with after-tax dollars, and then pay taxes again when you withdraw the savings in retirement. And if you lose your job or switch to a new one, the time frame to pay back the loan shrinks to as few as 60 days. If you can't pay the loan by the deadline, and you're younger than 59½, you could be hit with another tax bill and a 10 percent early withdrawal penalty.

So you might want to think about another plan, one that will help you sleep at night without agonizing about the sudden drop in your retirement savings.

Pay Off Your Student Loans

Student loans can feel like an insurmountable burden, but there are steps you can take to make paying down student debt more manageable. Here are just a few:

- You may be able to lengthen the time you have to pay the debt back, or consolidate your loans. To learn what repayment options are available to you, contact your lender or your current student loans holder.

- Pay as much as you can over the minimum to shorten the lifetime of your payments, and in turn reduce the interest you pay.

- If your kids are older and established in their careers, talk with them about assuming all or some of the debt payments for their education.

- If you're nearing retirement and have a child about to enter college or a child who's in college already, be sure to keep borrowing and spending for higher education in check. Your child can borrow or pay for his or her own college, but you can't borrow for retirement. You might also talk to them about getting a job while attending school, and how important it is for them to have some skin in the game. We all want to help our kids with college and expenses, and we don't want them to graduate and begin their adult life saddled with debt, but think about this: when you're elderly, out of funds, and relying on them for support, have you done them any favors in the long run?

We can't stress how important it is for you to look into these options.

Pay Off Your Credit Cards

Getting out from under a pile of debt can seem intimidating, but following these steps can help you do so as quickly and smoothly as possible.

Create a Clear Plan

Draft a timeline showing when you'll have each credit card's debt paid off. As you pay off each debt, track your progress on your timeline. When you feel like giving up, take a look at your chart. It helps you stay on track. When planning the order that you'll pay off your debt, be sure to put your highest interest rate credit card debt first. Pay as much as you can on that card every month, and pay the minimum on all your other debts. When you've paid off your top debt, prioritize paying your card with the second-highest interest rate, paying the same amount you had been paying toward the debt you've just paid off. At the same time, continue to pay the minimum on your other debts. Continue the process until all your debts are paid off, and then in the future, maintain a zero balance by paying off your card in full each month.

Create a Budget

Increasing your payments will help you get out of debt, but only if you're not racking up more debt at the same time. Let's face it, if you want to get out of debt, you have to live within your means by sticking to a budget. Not a mental budget, which can cause all kinds of mistakes, but a budget that shows you the hard numbers. Be honest about what you can afford to do. Creating an ambitious plan is great, but if your goals aren't realistic, you might get disheartened. If you find yourself with extra income—maybe from freelance work or overtime—write down exactly what you're putting that money toward, so you don't imagine it going farther than it actually will.

Ask Your Lender for Help

I know we conduct much of our day-to-day business online, but if you're overwhelmed by monthly payments, pick up the phone or set up a meeting to talk with the lender about a lower interest rate or a different payment plan to help you pay off your debt. Before you call, make sure you've prepared your explanation for needing help. When you meet, on the phone or in person, introduce yourself as a loyal customer, ask for assistance, and remain calm and friendly. If you don't seem to be getting anywhere with the person you're talking with, ask to talk to a supervisor or someone with the authority to help you out.

Avoid These Mistakes

Whether you've never been in debt, are digging your way out now, or have just dug your way out, here are a few steps you should not take.

Increasing Your Debt

We're not saying to tear up your credit cards. They're essential for certain items, such as booking flights, medical emergencies, and getting your roots done (ha!), but don't spend beyond your means every month and depend on your credit card to make up the difference. Sure, by whipping out your credit card for basics like groceries and gas you can earn reward points and even receive cash back, but you also rack up interest if you don't pay your card off at the end of the month. A good rule of thumb is to pull out the plastic only if you're positive you can and will pay off the balance at the end of the payment cycle.

Paying the Minimum Only

Try to pay your credit card in full every month. Paying the minimum is really tempting, but the practice will cost you a lot of money in interest fees in the long run. If you need to carry a balance, keep it as low as possible.

Paying Late

Always pay your credit card bills on time. Pay no less than the minimum, and whenever possible, pay in full. If you're constantly late or miss payments, you risk adding large penalties and lowering your credit score. For loan payments that stay the same each month, set up automatic payments with your bank. At the very least, set up a reminder of your payment due date on your calendar.

If you're usually on time but are struggling one month, you might be able to waive a late fee and a hit to your credit score by giving your lender a call ahead of time. But if you've got a history of late payments, the only way to begin cleaning up your credit report is to make up the payments you owe and start paying at least the minimum. On time. Every month.

Putting Your Credit Card Debt Last

Paying off credit card debt is even more important than paying your highest-interest-rate, non-credit card debt. While it may seem to make sense to pay off larger debts—your car loan or mortgage—and let your credit card payments slip, the financial hit could be heavier. Unlike fully amortized loans, like a 30-year mortgage, where you pay off the principal (amount of loan) plus interest in regular installments, credit card debt is revolving. This means that if you don't pay off your balance in full at the end of the month, the amount you owe grows as interest accrues. In other words, you pay interest today on not only your principal balance, but also on the interest you were previously charged. So even if your car loan charges more interest than your credit card, take care of the card first.

Start Paying Yourself

With so much uncertainty in today's economy and the rising cost of health insurance premiums and college tuition, reducing debt goes a long way to feeling you have some control over your finances, finances you'll need to help guard against decreases in employer- and government-funded retirement programs like pensions and Social Security. So instead of paying interest to someone else for past purchases, pay off your debt and start putting those interest payments aside for your retirement, so you can enjoy the retirement you've been looking forward to.

KEY POINTS

- Avoid carrying large amounts of debt into retirement. It can impact the retirement funds available for day-to-day living and emergency expenses.

- If you're not yet retired, avoid dipping into your retirement to pay off debt.

- To manage debt, make a realistic plan, create a budget, and stick to both.

- Whenever possible, do not increase your debt. Pay the minimum balance on your credit card, pay on time, and put your credit card first.

HEALTHCARE

WE EXPECT OUR EXPENSES to decrease in our post-retirement years. We'll shell out less for gas because we're not driving to work every day or hauling the kids around. We may have paid off our mortgages. We won't need to devote a percentage of our budget to business attire. So sure, some expenses will go down, but healthcare will probably not be one of them. In fact, the opposite is true—the longer we live, and we are living longer, the greater our need for healthcare.

As we age, we're more likely to need help for chronic conditions and long-term care. Just take a look at the very basics—hearing aids, eye glasses, possibly dentures. Nearly 25 percent of those aged 65–74 and 50 percent of those who are 75 and older have disabling hearing loss.[1] Ninety-three percent of people 65–75 years of age wear corrective lenses.[2] And American Dental Association surveys show that 50 percent of people age 55 and older wear partial or complete dentures.[3]

Who's paying for it all? In the past, large businesses often paid retirees' health insurance, but not anymore. Today, we have to rely on Medicare for a huge portion of our coverage, but rapidly increasing healthcare costs and our aging population have put the future of Medicare in jeopardy, increasing the need for supplemental coverage. The situation is not going to get better anytime soon—healthcare costs will continue to rise at a much greater rate than our other expenses.

Rising Costs

Almost 20 percent of the US economy is devoted to healthcare spending, and that percentage continues to rise every year.[2]

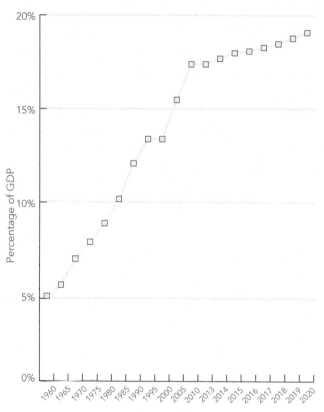

National Health Expenditures as a Percentage of Gross Domestic Product

Source: Centers for Medicare and Medicaid Services

In 2013, that amounted to an average of $9,225 per person for healthcare. That's 50 percent higher than 10 years earlier, when it was $6,132, and nearly three times more than the 1990 level of $2,854.[4] From 2000–2013, healthcare spending per person grew at an average rate of nearly 6 percent a year—much higher than the 2.4 percent inflation rate. Wouldn't it be great if the economy were growing as much as healthcare spending? The worst part is that of the estimated $2.9 trillion we spend annually on healthcare, experts agree that approximately 20–30 percent of that spending—up to $800 billion a year—goes to care that is wasteful, redundant, or inefficient, such as unnecessary tests, brand-name drugs, and the latest and greatest equipment the public demands.[5]

National Health Expenditures per Capita

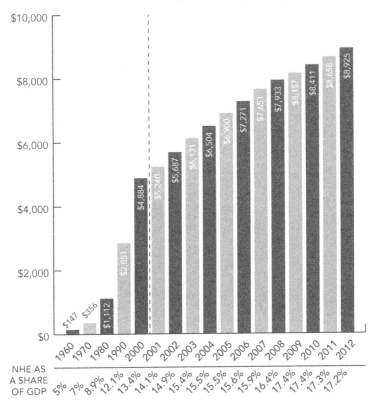

Source: Kaiser Family Foundation calculations using NHE data from Centers for Medicare and Medicaid Services, Office of the Actuary, National Health Statistics Group

As a result of the rising costs, the share of our national economy devoted to healthcare grew from 7.0 percent in 1970 to 17.4 percent in 2013.[6] By the year 2020, the Centers for Medicare and Medicaid Services projects that health spending will be 19.3 percent, nearly one-fifth of our gross domestic product.[7] So as you budget for your retirement, in addition to accounting for inflation, you'll need to account for the percentage of your budget devoted to healthcare.

Just how much do you need to save for healthcare in retirement? In 2000, healthcare spending for older married couples was 16 percent of their total income. That number increased to 24 percent by 2010. It's expected to increase to 29 percent in 2020 and 35 percent in 2030.[8]

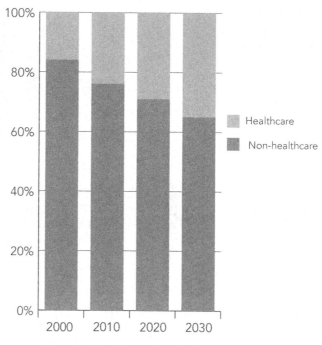

Healthcare as a Percentage of 65-Year-Old Couple's Income

Source: Administration on Aging (AoA).
Projections of Future Growth of the Older Population. December 31, 2010.

What does this mean for those who are planning to retire or have retired? The soaring cost of medical care means less money in already stretched budgets, and can force tough choices about balancing food, rent/mortgage, and needed care.

Why have US healthcare costs risen so dramatically?

- We live in a nation in love with lawsuits, so medical providers need to practice defensive medicine to cover themselves. That cost is passed on to us.

- We've become used to receiving the latest and greatest technology without considering effectiveness, so our costs reflect this preference.

- The cost of developing a drug keeps increasing. Today, the cost is approximately $2.6 billion per drug.[9] And some of these new medicines may be no more effective than older, less costly ones. The result? Many seniors can't afford these drugs, so some take less than the prescribed amount and some don't even fill their prescriptions.

  - In 2014, a poll found that 31 percent of those polled did not fill at least one prescription in the last year because of cost.[10]

  - A study in 2003 found that 17 percent had taken a prescription drug in smaller doses than prescribed because of the cost.[11]

Another contributing factor is that providers are merging, creating huge monopolies. Our hospitals and other providers are increasingly gaining market share and are better able to demand higher prices. While mergers or partnerships among medical providers or insurers may improve efficiency and help drive down prices, consolidation can also have the opposite effect, allowing near-monopolies in some markets and driving up prices. Increasingly, hospitals are buying up rivals, creating larger medical systems.

Then there's our general health. As a nation, we're not in the best shape. In 2012, nearly half the US population had one or more chronic conditions—including heart disease and diabetes—which drive up healthcare costs.[12] And more than one-third of all adults are obese, which can directly lead to the former conditions in addition to other chronic illnesses, which leads to even more medical spending.[13]

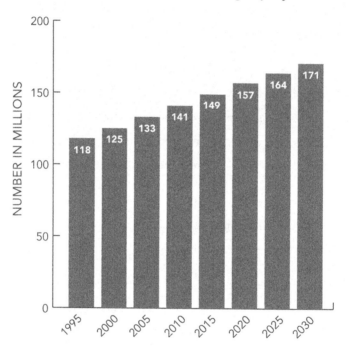

The Number of People with Chronic Conditions Is Rising Rapidly

Source: Robert Woods Johnson Foundation.
"Chronic Care: Making the Case for Ongoing Care," February 2010.

According to the Centers for Disease Control and Prevention, our common, health-damaging but modifiable behaviors—tobacco use, insufficient physical activity, poor eating habits, and excessive alcohol use—are responsible for much of the illness, disability, and premature death related to chronic disease. Approximately 84 percent of all healthcare spending and 99 percent of all Medicare spending in the United States is for the 50 percent of the population who have one or more chronic medical conditions.[14]

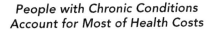

**People with Chronic Conditions
Account for Most of Health Costs**

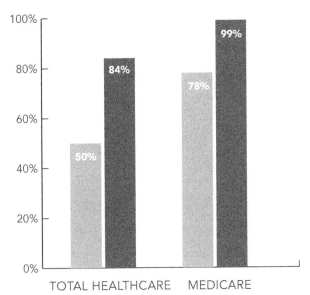

Percentage of Non-institutionalized Population with ≥ 1 Chronic Condition
Percentage of Spending on People with Chronic Conditions

Source: The Robert Wood Johnson Foundation.
"Chronic Care: Making the Case for Ongoing Care," February 2010.

Medicare Is in Trouble

America's population is aging, and the aged use greater healthcare services. From 2007, the percentage of the population that is 65 and older has been gradually increasing and will continue to increase until it nearly doubles, reaching a rate of greater than 20 percent of the population by the year 2050.[15] The older people become, the more likely they will need medical services. That's just a fact of life.

The aging population, combined with people's longer lifespans, means more people will utilize Medicare and Medicaid entitlement program benefits and for longer periods of time.

Approximately 52 million Americans were covered by Medicare in 2013, at a cost of approximately $583 billion, or about 3.6 percent of the nation's gross domestic product.[16] By 2024, approximately 70 million people will receive healthcare paid for by Medicare, and their tab is expected to hit $858 billion.[17] Without changes to the Medicare system, Medicare costs could grow to 9.8 percent of GDP by 2087. Changes need to be made, because without them, the HI Medicare Trust Fund balance could be exhausted by 2029.[18]

Although Medicare is the third-largest item in the federal budget, many Americans are unaware that it is one of the biggest budget items. Plus, most Americans don't see Medicare spending as a major contributor to the deficit today. One reason that many people believe Medicare does not contribute to the deficit is that the majority think Medicare recipients pay or have pre-paid the cost of their healthcare. It's just not true. Medicare beneficiaries on average pay only approximately one dollar for every three dollars in benefits they receive. However, roughly two-thirds of Americans believe that most Medicare recipients get benefits worth about the same as or less than what they have paid in payroll taxes during their working lives and in premiums for their current coverage.[19]

As you create your retirement plan, you'll want to take a close look at the benefits Medicare provides, and take into account that the costs will rise and the benefits could decrease, which means you'll pay more out of pocket. You want to plan for that so you won't be caught short.

Planning for Long-Term Care

Since we wrote the first chapter of this book, Nancy's mom, who has diabetes, had to have her leg amputated. It's been horrible for us all, but especially for her. Since Nancy's mom doesn't have a penny to her name, Medicaid covered her amputation and her recovery in a nursing home. Let us tell you, she hated it there. She hated the stale, antiseptic smell, and she hated the building—old with gray walls and worn linoleum. It was extremely depressing, with absolutely no frills. It was not a place you'd want to spend a lot of time in. And she didn't.

Since she'll have a long road to recovery, Nancy and her brother have had to move her into a private nursing home. The cost of 24-hour care in her assisted living facility was just too expensive. It was a hard adjustment, but we all had to face it.

None of us want our parents to be in the position Nancy's mom is in. And none of us want to think we'll be there. We sure don't. Our go-to mindset is, *We won't need long-term care. We'll beat those odds. We eat really well. We go to the gym.* First of all, long-term care doesn't necessarily mean a nursing home. Long-term care is a range of services and supports you may need to meet your personal care needs. Most long-term care is not medical care; it's assistance with the basic personal tasks of everyday life—bathing, dressing, toilet use, moving to and from bed, and eating. Other common long-term care services and supports provide assistance with everyday tasks such as housework, taking medication, meal preparation and cleaning, shopping, pet care, and money management.

Here's the thing—most long-term care services are not covered by health insurance, long-term disability insurance (which replaces a portion of lost wages due to illnesses or accidents that meet the policy's definition for benefit eligibility), Medicare, or Medicare supplemental coverage.

Here's an example of how Medicare works for long-term care:

- Medicare pays for skilled care in a nursing home only for the short period during which you're recuperating from a hospital stay (up to 100 days).

- Once your care needs stabilize, Medicare won't pay for personal or custodial care, even if you need these services.

- If you need at-home care, Medicare will pay only under very limited circumstances. Medicaid only pays for long-term care for seniors based on financial need.

- If you have money, you need to go through all of it. When you're destitute, you'll qualify for Medicaid.

What Are the Odds of Needing Care?

Let's get back to how many seniors will need some type of long-term care. Seventy percent of people turning 65 years of age can expect to use some form of long-term care during their lives. There are a number of factors that can influence whether you might need care.

The older you are, the more likely you will need long-term care. Your gender plays a part too. Some refer to long-term care is a woman's issue, and they're not entirely wrong—women outlive men by an average of five years, so they're more likely to live at home alone when they're older. Seventy-one percent of claims dollars are paid to female claimants. Anyone who's ever been to visit in a nursing home might think the proportion is higher than that, since women make up around 80 percent or more of all nursing home residents.[20]

The duration and level of long-term care will vary from person to person and often change over time. Here are some statistics to consider:

- Someone turning age 65 today has almost a 70 percent chance of needing some type of long-term care services and support in their remaining years.

- As a general rule, women need care longer (3.7 years) than men (2.2 years).

- One-third of today's 65-year-olds may never need long-term care support, but 20 percent will need it for longer than five years.[21]

What Does Long-Term Care Cost?

Many people don't realize that Medicare doesn't usually cover long-term care. And long-term care can be expensive. Lengthy assisted living or nursing home stays can decimate even the best-laid retirement plan. In addition to the financial costs of care, there's also an emotional cost on family and friends as they struggle to support and assist their loved one. It's extremely stressful. Providing care for Nancy's mom sure caused tension among the siblings. A family may be willing to provide care, but you have to consider the physical and emotional cost.

In 2014, long-term care in the United States cost on average:

- $212 per day or $6,448 per month ($77,380 per year) for a semi-private room in a nursing home

- $240 per day or $7,300 per month ($87,360 per year) for a private room in a nursing home

- $3,500 per month ($42,000 per year) for a one-bedroom unit in an assisted living facility

- $20 per hour for a home health aide

- $19 per hour for homemaker services, such as bill pay, medications, home care, shopping

- $65 per day for services in an adult day healthcare center.[22]

Long-Term Health Costs

TYPE OF CARE	NATIONAL MEDIAN RATE
Homemaker services	$19 (hourly)
Home health aide services	$20 (hourly)
Adult health day care (ADC)	$65 (daily)
Assisted living facility (ALF)	$3,500 (monthly)
Nursing home care (semiprivate)	$212 (daily)
Nursing home care (private)	$240 (daily)

Source: Genworth 2014 Cost of Care Survey

Help Is Here

Only long-term care insurance covers the type of day-to-day personal care assistance you might need if you are unable to care for yourself as a result of chronic illness, disability, or disease. Long-term care insurance provides a daily cash benefit to cover the costs of healthcare services provided in a nursing home, your own home, an assisted living facility, or an adult day care facility. This type of care is known as personal or custodial care.

Long-term care insurance can help you:

- Maintain your independence, so you won't have to rely on family members

- Protect your assets against the high costs of long-term care, better preserving your children's inheritance

- Make long-term care services affordable, such as home healthcare and custodial care

- Provide yourself with more options than just nursing home care

- Pay for nursing home care if it's needed

- Preserve your standard of living

Making sure all the costs of your care—emotional and financial—are taken care of can bring such peace of mind, allowing you to focus on living your life as independently as possible.

KEY POINTS

- **Healthcare costs are rising and will continue to rise. Out-of-pocket expenses will increase, so when planning for retirement, remember to take into account these costs.**

- **Long-term care is vital to your retirement planning. It's a good idea to start sooner than later, so contact your financial advisor about which plan will work for you.**

TAXES

YOU PROBABLY KNOW a lot of this information, but we have to let you know—government taxes can eat up much of what you've worked so hard to save, and taxes may rise even higher, including taxes on Social Security benefits. Here are some of the landmines that trip people up.

Taxes on Your Retirement Savings

Here's a fairly common story about a man who graduated college in the early 1970s with a BA in liberal arts—a popular degree at the time. He helped put himself through school by working weekends on the ski patrol at the ski area 30 minutes from his off-campus apartment. He loved all things sports, so when he graduated, he took an entry-level sales position at a well-known sporting goods chain. Eventually, he managed the ski department, and then worked his way up to overseeing several stores.

A few years out of college, he got married. His wife spent many years of their married life taking care of the kids and writing freelance for a local newspaper. Because she worked part-time, she had no retirement benefits, but he did, so they felt they were in good shape. From the day he started at the sporting goods store, his parents' words ringing in his ears, he made sure to make a full contribution to his company's 401(k), the amount matched by his employer. When he could, he also put money toward his IRA. He and his wife had bills to pay, kids to feed and clothe, and a mortgage to meet, so deferring taxes made good sense to them. When they retired, their income would be much lower, they reasoned, so their taxes would be non-existent. They were wrong.

By the time the couple was ready to retire, they'd paid off their mortgage, cut back on their expenses, and planned on enjoying the good life, traveling together. But when they sat down with their financial advisor to discuss their retirement plan, how much they could take out each month, they realized taxes were far greater than they'd planned. So here they are—high taxes and no deductions, and they have to rethink their retirement strategy.

We're not advising against putting your money in a 401(k). If your employer matches your contribution, it's smart to put aside a portion of your paycheck to receive the maximum matching funds from your employer. However, putting aside more than your employer will match may not be the best way to put aside money for your retirement. You'll want to talk with your financial advisor about which strategy might be best for your retirement plan.

In addition to your 401(k) contribution, you want to put any money you can toward retirement. If your employer does not offer a retirement package, you need to put even more aside. An IRA is considered a good bet. Many, like the couple above, want to stash away the allowable amount toward an IRA each year to save taxes. However, there are two types of IRAs—traditional (contributions are not taxed going in but they are going out) and Roth (contributions are taxed going in but not going out). As with everything else, there are plusses and minuses to each—and you want to research which one is right for you. You also want to explore other options to diversify your retirement.

Traditional IRA

With a traditional IRA, you save on taxes on the front end when you contribute to your IRA, and pay them on the back end when you withdraw. It's just good strategy: increase your retirement savings and decrease your taxes. Then again, maybe it's not. At least not always. Sure you get to save on taxes going in, but there are also disadvantages, particularly these days, when people are working longer to supplement their retirement income, and their income tax rates don't go down. Or when taxes may climb higher than you anticipated going in.

Here are a few ins and outs of traditional IRAs:

- You must meet the eligibility requirements to qualify for tax benefits.

- All withdrawals from a traditional IRA are included in gross income and are subject to federal income tax.

- Unless you meet some exception allowed by the IRS, you will be subject to a 10 percent penalty if you withdraw your money before age 59½.

- Taxes (and maybe penalties) must be paid before cash in the account can be withdrawn and used, so this account is harder to use for emergencies.

- The IRS doesn't want your money to remain tax-free forever, so there are rules about how long you can keep your money stashed away in your IRA. According to a formula put out by the IRS, you have to start taking withdrawals six months past your seventieth birthday. This is called the Required Minimum Distribution (RMD). If you don't make the required withdrawals, the IRS will automatically deduct a penalty of 50 percent of the amount you're required to withdraw. If you want to keep your money in an account a bit longer to let it grow, you can't—there are only a few exceptions. The mandatory withdrawal also prevents you from keeping the money in your traditional IRA for your children to inherit. The mandatory withdrawals create taxable income for you whether you want it or not, and can cause you to have to pay tax on your Social Security benefits.

Roth IRAs

Roth IRAs can be a solution to a traditional IRA's disadvantages. With a Roth IRA, you pay taxes going in and not when you withdraw, when paying out those taxes may be more of a hardship. There are two requirements to be able to withdraw. First, you must wait at least five years after putting your money in, and second, you must have a justification for your withdrawal; for example, your retirement or a disability. Reaching 59½ years of age is the simplest justification, at which point you can make qualified withdrawals in any amount on any schedule.

Here are a few factors to consider when deciding if a Roth IRA is right for you:

- If you're in the prime of your career and your earnings put you in the maximum tax bracket, the value of getting a tax deduction on traditional retirement-account contributions is extremely high. So using a Roth and giving up that deduction doesn't make much sense.

- If your income (and your tax rate) is low, it might make more sense to pay taxes now (Roth IRA) rather than defer them (traditional IRA).

- You risk tax laws changing over the course of decades. When you contribute to a traditional IRA, you're guaranteed to realize an immediate tax benefit. When you contribute to a Roth IRA, you have to wait for a number of years before realizing the tax benefit. If laws allowing for a tax-free withdrawal change during the interim, and some analysts fear they will, you may not only lose the tax benefit up front, but you could end up having to pay taxes at the end too.

- Since you've paid the taxes up front, and you don't have to withdraw your funds after you reach age 70½, you can leave tax-free income to your loved ones or organizations that can grow during their lifetime if they choose to leave the money in the account.

- Taxable income from a traditional IRA can cause you to pay taxes on your Social Security benefits, whereas income from a Roth IRA will not.

You don't necessarily have to pick one or the other. You might want to take a conservative approach and contribute to both to hedge your bets for the future. You could contribute to your traditional IRA until you reach the contribution limit, and then contribute additional funds to a Roth IRA. If you have a traditional IRA, there might be advantages for you in converting it to a Roth IRA. Talk with your financial advisor.

SEP IRA

A Simplified Employee Pension Individual Retirement Arrangement (SEP IRA) is a variation of the traditional IRA. If you own a business, you could set up a SEP IRA to provide retirement benefits for you and your employees (on a discretionary basis). If you have no employees, you can still set up a SEP IRA for yourself. You're allowed a tax deduction for all contributions you make to your SEP plan and to your employees' SEP plans. Funds can be allocated the same way as most other IRAs.

Stretch IRA

A stretch IRA is an option that allows you to extend the financial life of an IRA to a future generation. It can be applied to both traditional and Roth IRAs. The strategy allows you to pass on assets to a designated second-generation or even a third- or fourth-generation beneficiary while allowing them to enjoy the benefits of tax-deferred and/or tax-free growth as long as possible. Stretching out an IRA gives the funds in the IRA more time—potentially decades—to grow without having taxes taken out, which provides the opportunity to grow the funds significantly. The required minimum annual distribution (RMD) is calculated based on life expectancy. So the younger the beneficiary, the lower the RMD, which allows more funds to remain in the IRA to stretch the IRA over time.

Social Security Taxes

On the whole, Americans are counting on their Social Security checks to cover certain expenses. But here's the thing: you may have to hand part of your benefit back to the government in the form of taxes. For example, taxable income from a traditional IRA can cause you to pay taxes on your Social Security benefits.

About 15 million Americans pay income taxes on their Social Security benefits—a surprise for many seniors, whether continuing to work or not, who were planning on a source of tax-free income. Depending on your income, you could pay tax on up to 50 or 85 percent of your benefits.

History

Originally, the benefits received by retirees were not taxed as income, but in the late 1970s, Congress appointed a Social Security Advisory Council to look into how to fund Social Security to withstand the massive benefits

due to the approaching boomer drain. They decided they needed to tax
Social Security income as a way of dealing with the shortfall.

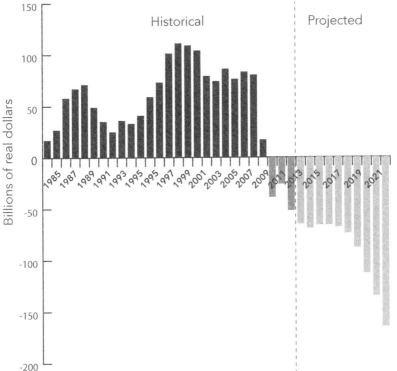

Social Security Trust Fund's Annual Cash Flows

Source: 2013 Social Security Trustees Report, Congressional Budget Office, Veronique de Rugy,
Mercatus Center at George Mason University

Will Your Social Security Be Taxable?

Unfortunately, there's a good chance it will. As you prepare for retirement, it's
essential to determine if your benefits will be tax-free or vulnerable to a tax hit.
The first step is to compute your provisional income, which is basically your
adjusted gross income (not counting any Social Security benefits) plus any
tax-exempt interest and 50 percent of your Social Security benefits. So provisional income = adjusted income + tax-exempt interest + 50% of SS benefits.

If your provisional income is less than $25,000 annually ($32,000 for couples filing jointly), then your benefits aren't taxable.

- If your provisional income is between $25,000 and $34,000 ($32,000 to $44,000 for couples), then you could have to pay income tax on up to 50 percent of your benefits. The amount included in taxable income is either half of your benefits or half of the amount by which provisional income exceeds the $25,000 lower limit, whichever is less.

- If your provisional income is more than $34,000 ($44,000 for couples), then you could have to pay income tax on up to 85 percent of your benefit. The amount included in taxable income is either 85 percent of your benefits or 85 percent of the amount that exceeds the limit for joint returns.

Potential Tax Payments at 50% Lower Limit

STATUS	AMOUNT
Your provisional income (income + ½ SS)	$38,000
Amount of SS benefits	$8,000
½ of income over $32,000 lower limit	$3,000
½ of SS benefits	$4,000
Amount to be taxed	$3,000
Possible tax due	$450

So what if you fall in a higher-income bracket? Maybe you plan to keep working. Let's say your provisional income is $80,000 and you and your spouse receive a total of $25,000 in benefits. 85 percent of your social security benefits ($21,250) would be taxed, costing you $5,312.50 in extra federal income tax in the 25-percent bracket. This hit could be a shock.

Potential Tax Payments at 85% Lower Limit

STATUS	AMOUNT
Your provisional income (income + ½ SS)	$80,000
Amount of SS benefits	$25,000
85% of income over $44,000 lower limit	$30,600
85% of SS benefits	$21,250
Amount to be taxed	$21,250
Possible tax due	$5,312.50

The good news is you won't ever have to pay income tax on 100 percent of your Social Security income. There are many ways to avoid Uncle Sam's reach. The simplest way is to keep your expenses low, so you don't need as much income, but that's not always easy because medical expenses increase as you age and you need money to cover them. Another way to avoid Uncle Sam is to diversify your retirement income. For example, you can withdraw $5,000 per year from a Roth IRA, and it won't change any of the calculations above. Roth IRA distributions—withdrawals from a Roth IRA—do not affect your Social Security in any way. There are many steps you can take to reduce taxes that you do pay. Consult your financial expert about your options.

Life Planning

We heard a story about a man who served in the army during WWII. He was in the Pacific Theater. For part of his tour of duty, he worked for a popular military magazine, setting type on the printing press. When he returned home, he set up a print shop and started churning out flyers and copy for local businesses. A few months later, a friend introduced him to a woman who would soon be his wife. She was a widow whose husband had been killed in the war, and she was raising her four-year-old boy on her own. She was tough and funny, and her husband-to-be was hooked from the moment he saw her. On their first date, they went out dancing at the Vets Club. A few months later they married, and he adopted her son.

The couple built a house together, with their son helping with age-appropriate jobs—digging holes for hydrangeas, for one. Over the years, the print business provided them with a good income. Having grown up during the Great Depression, they were frugal, but not enough to save significantly. They always planned on funding their retirement by selling the shop. The husband worked well into his seventies before he retired. When he did, the digital age had arrived, and his shop, with its outdated equipment, brought some money (he still had loyal clients) but not nearly as much as he'd hoped. Still, if the couple tightened their belts, they would be okay. They could stay in their home and leave their house to their son and his family when they died.

He died when he was 83. His wife, 80, was the beneficiary of his will. Their son did what he could to help his mother out around the house, but, finally, she decided to move to a retirement community, which cost more than she had in savings. So she sold her home, still hoping to leave something to her son and his family, who repeatedly told her to spend the money on herself. She passed away a few years later. When she died, the government took half her savings—taxes—and she was able to leave her son and her grandchildren only a small portion of what she and her husband had planned.

With some sound advice and planning, the couple could have checked out a number of retirement plans that would have allowed them to have a more enjoyable retirement and leave more to their son. In the next chapter, you'll learn more about how to avoid these pitfalls, as well as some of the options available to you.

KEY POINTS

- Don't forget to plan for taxes to take a large bite out of your retirement income.

- When it comes to your 401(k), allocating more than your employer will match is generally not your best option.

- There are two types of IRAs—traditional and Roth. Each has advantages and disadvantages, so you need to explore which one will work for you.

- Your Social Security benefits may be taxed. You need to take this possibility into consideration when planning your retirement.

RETIREMENT SOLUTIONS

ONE OF THE REASONS we chose to write this book was to bring awareness to the financial crisis so many families are facing in the near future—people are living longer, planning less, and government coffers are stretched. But we also wanted to give you hope that, if planned correctly, it's never too late to begin the task of financially protecting you and your loved ones from the impact. We've discussed how some financial strategies may or may not be the best answer to secure your future. We've also talked about consistency. Set an amount you can live with, then put that amount toward your retirement each and every month. Consistency pays off. Consistency is what builds any savings plan, including an insurance plan.

This chapter will discuss concepts that could favorably alter the financial and retirement crisis we all face. Regardless of your situation, many insurance products of today shared in this chapter can be very helpful with your financial planning. We'll give you a snapshot of some basic insurance solutions for retirement, long-term care, and leaving your assets to your beneficiaries. And for those of you who may have a business, we've even added a section about how to protect that business for you and your loved ones. See what might work for you or just get an idea of what's out there, then contact your financial advisor to help determine a plan for the safe, secure retirement you deserve.

Personal Life Insurance

Life insurance is critical for keeping your loved ones safe and cared for, with their lives intact. However, life insurance can do much more than protect your family if you or your partner die. Life insurance can also help with retirement, long-term care, and planning how to leave your assets— no matter how large or small—to your loved ones or organizations.

There are two major types of life insurance: term life insurance and permanent life insurance, which includes whole life and universal life. We'll discuss each one in this chapter.

Term Life

This type of policy provides protection for a specified period of time (usually 10–30 years). Unlike whole life insurance and universal life insurance, term life insurance does not build cash value. That means, you buy a policy for a specific, or fixed, death benefit, and the policy pays the fixed death benefit only when the policy holder dies within the time the policy is active. Why might you choose this policy? You can buy a greater amount of insurance at lower rates, because the insurance lasts only for a specified period. When your policy expires, if you want to take out another policy—say you bought it at 25, you're now 55, and you'd still like coverage for mortgage and college—your rates will be higher.

Some term life products include a living benefits rider (an addition to your policy). This rider allows you to receive benefits from your life insurance policy before you die. This can help you deal with the expenses related to events such as terminal or catastrophic illnesses and long-term care. The life insurance company will deduct the amount of living benefits paid to you from the policy's death benefit.

There are three basic types of term insurance.

Adjustable renewal and convertible policies provide protection for one year. You can renew the policy for successive periods thereafter, but at higher premiums without having to furnish evidence of insurability.

Level term policies have an initial guaranteed premium level for specified periods. The longer the guarantee, the greater the cost (but usually still far more affordable than permanent policies). These policies may be renewed after the guarantee period, but the premiums *do* increase as the insured gets older.

Decreasing term policies have a level premium, but the amount of the death benefit decreases with time. These policies are often used in conjunction with mortgage debt protection.

Tax Facts

There are minimal consequences unless you sell a policy to a third party. If you do, capital gains or ordinary income tax may apply, depending on the type of sale and the rules applying to cost basis.

Is Term Life for You?

Term life might be for you if you have a large mortgage that needs to be paid, children who are counting on you for college funding, or a spouse who couldn't replace your salary.

Key Features of Term Life Insurance

FEATURE	DETAILS
Protection	Limited to a fixed period
Premium cost	Less than whole life
Savings feature	No cash value accumulation
Loans	No loans are permitted
Tax benefits	None
Renewability	Yes
Premium increases	Likely, if policy is renewed for another period
Policy types	Adjustable renewal & convertible Level term Decreasing term

Permanent Life Insurance

Unlike term life insurance, which provides coverage for a set period of time, permanent life insurance provides coverage for your entire life.

Whole Life

Insurance premiums are typically higher on whole life policies than most other types of life insurance and can be paid as a single lump payment or over a period of time. This type of policy combines a fixed death benefit, an amount determined when you take out the policy, and builds up cash value during the life of your policy. Whole life policies can include a living benefits rider.

EXAMPLE

Here's how it works. Each month, you pay the premium, which is more than you need to cover insurance costs and expenses. The insurance company applies the additional funds toward a cash value account. In other words, the company invests the additional funds in their portfolio. Your account value fluctuates based on the state of the investment markets, such as stocks and bonds. However, you're guaranteed a certain amount to protect against a low market. If you live to reach the policy's maturity date, the insurance company will pay only the death benefit to you. They keep the accumulated cash value (equal at maturity to the death benefit) unless you deplete it when you die.

SINGLE PREMIUM LIFE

Single premium life (SPL) is a form of whole life insurance, where you pay a lump sum up front for a determined death payment when you die. The death benefit is guaranteed to remain paid-up until you die. With SPL, the cash value can build up more quickly because you've paid the policy in full.

So if you have extra cash, with SPL, you can pass on money to your family or a charity tax-free. It can give you tax-free access to the death benefit if you need to pay for long-term care expenses. With this policy, you can access your cash value for emergencies, retirement, or other opportunities by taking loans or withdrawals subject to certain restrictions. If you decide to take a loan or withdrawal, first talk with your financial advisor about the tax consequences.

EXAMPLE

The following example illustrates the difference between how a single premium life policy and a CD might pay out. The insured is a female, sixty-two years of age. She's a non-smoker with $50,000 earmarked for her grandchildren. She is concerned about health-related expenses during her lifetime, such as medical costs or nursing home care.

Amounts to Grandchildren at Insured's Death

CD Deposit	50,000
Estimated Rate of Return	1.0%
Age When Purchased	65
Gender	Female
Tax Bracket	28%
Single Premium	$50,000
Life Insurance Death Benefit	$92,674

YEAR AFTER PURCHASE	BEFORE TAX VALUE OF CD	AFTER TAX VALUE OF CD	LIFE INSURANCE DEATH BENEFIT
0	$50,000	—	$92,764
5	$52,564	$51,846	$92,764
10	$55,258	$53,786	$92,764
15	$58,092	$56,109	$92,764
20	$61,070	$58,985	$92,764
25	$64,201	$62,010	$92,764

This proposal is intended for value purposes only. It assumes a hypothetical rate of interest and taxable amount for a certificate of deposit that's not guaranteed. CD rate is compounded daily. A certificate of deposit is a bank product and insured by the FDIC or NCUA. Comments here reflect our understanding of the current tax law. Laws are subject to different interpretations and changes. Consult with your personal advisor for additional guidance.

This is a value comparison using an assumed one-time single premium amount to fund a life insurance policy. Only funds not needed for daily living should be used to pay the single premium. The additional amount available at death from a single premium whole life product may be greater than the assumed after tax earnings and principal from a certificate of deposit over the projected period of time shown. Life insurance products are not FDIC or NCUA insured. Life insurance death benefits are generally paid income tax free.

IS WHOLE LIFE FOR YOU?

Whole life could be for you if you want protection for your whole life, the guarantee of having the same premium for life, the ability to draw on the cash value of the policy as you get older, and another option for a tax-free retirement strategy.

Key Features of Whole Life Insurance

FEATURE	DETAILS
Protection	Lifetime (does not expire)
Premium cost	Most expensive
Savings feature	Builds cash value
Loans	Loans are permitted against cash value
Tax benefits	Favorable tax treatment on earnings
Renewability	Yes
Premium increases	Level through life of policy
Policy types	• Single premium: You pay a lump sum up front for a determined death payment. That payment is guaranteed to remain paid-up until you die. • Level premium: A rate is established based on your age at the time of your purchase, and generally remains at a constant until you die.

Universal Life

Universal life is a type of permanent life insurance with a death benefit and/or a cash value account. There are several types of universal life policies: flexible premium life, guaranteed universal life, index, and variable universal.

Flexible premium life is similar to whole life insurance in that the cash value is held in the insurance company's general portfolio—you don't get to choose how the account is allocated. Unlike traditional whole life insurance, universal life insurance allows you flexibility in making premium payments—you can take money out of your cash value and use it toward your premium.

The insurer will generally provide very broad premium guidelines (minimum and maximum premium payments), but within these guidelines, you can choose how much and when you pay premiums. You're also free to change the policy's death benefit directly (again, within the limits set out by the policy) as your financial circumstances change. However, if you want to raise the amount of coverage, you'll need to go through the insurability process again, probably including a new medical exam, and your premiums will increase. Also, you can withdraw from the policy, but you may pay a greater than expected premium. Flexible premium life policies can include a living benefits rider.

Guaranteed universal life insurance provides a guaranteed death benefit even if the cash value drops significantly or there is no cash value remaining. Some may build some cash value, but most policies won't let you access your funds the way you can with a whole life policy. Premiums are typically lower than a whole life product, but higher than term. Guaranteed universal life policies can include a living benefits rider.

Index universal life insurance offers death benefit protection plus premium flexibility and adjustable death benefit. An indexed universal life insurance policy gives you the opportunity to allocate cash value amounts to either a fixed account (an account that earns interest based on an amount set by the company) or an equity index account (earnings paid with the value of the market). Typically these policies have a guarantee on the principal amount in the indexed account. That is, you're protected in a downward market, and there is a cap on the maximum return. Index universal life insurance policies can include a living benefits rider.

Variable universal life insurance also offers death benefit protection with premium flexibility and adjustable death benefits. This type of insurance is generally the most expensive type of cash value insurance because it allows you to allocate a portion of your premium to a separate account, which consists of various different types of investments within the insurer's portfolio, such as bonds. Risks are regulated by the federal security laws. With a variable universal life policy, you can withdraw from the cash value during your lifetime. Variable universal life insurance policies can include a living benefits rider.

IS UNIVERSAL LIFE FOR YOU?

Universal life might be for you if you want to tailor your policy to individual circumstances to provide the greatest benefit at any stage in life. However, universal life insurance policies do carry higher risk because of fluctuations in financial environment and interest rates that affect the cash value. You'll want to speak to your financial advisor about which type of universal life insurance would work best for your circumstances.

FEATURE	FLEXIBLE PREMIUM	GUARANTEED UNIVERSAL LIFE	INDEX UNIVERSAL LIFE	VARIABLE UNIVERSAL LIFE
Coverage	Up to lifetime	Up to lifetime	Up to lifetime	Up to lifetime
Premiums	Flexible, based on sufficient cash value	Flexible, based on sufficient cash value	Flexible, based on sufficient cash value	Flexible, based on sufficient cash value
Cash value accumulation	Cash value is held in the insurance company's general portfolio—so they, rather than you, choose how the account is allocated	Little, and possibly no, cash value. Interest rate set by the insurance company.	Linked to various investment market indexes. Gains are locked in annually.	Cash value can be invested in separate fund sub-accounts of your choosing— such as mutual funds and stocks and bonds.
Risk	Entirely on policy holder. Insurer does not guarantee any interest rate or cash value unless the money is invested in a fixed-income account.	Minimal. Companies provide a constant rate.	Moderate. Companies typically provide a minimum-rate floor, which is usually combined with a maximum-rate ceiling.	Entirely on policy holder. Insurer does not guarantee any interest rate or cash value unless the money is invested in a fixed-income account.
Guaranteed death benefit	Policy is based on cash value. Because of this, policy can expire early, pay out a reduced death benefit, or require increased premium payment. Increased cash value can provide the option of increased death benefit.	No-lapse feature—a promise to stay in effect for the guaranteed period (usually the insured's life) if the premium is paid regularly and on time, even if the cash value has run out.	Policy is based on cash value. Because of this, policy can expire early, pay out a reduced death benefit, or require increased premium payment. Increased cash value can provide the option of increased death benefit.	Policy is based on cash value. Because of this, policy can expire early, pay out a reduced death benefit, or require increased premium payment. Increased cash value can provide the option of increased death benefit.

POLICY REVIEW

Time changes, people change, needs change. So it's critical to review your life insurance policy with your agent once a year to answer these questions about your policy.

- Is the policy still the best for you?

- Does the policy provide the right amount of coverage?

- Is your policy still doing the job originally intended?

- Is your policy still priced competitively?

- Are there improvements you can make on your existing policy?

- Are there any upcoming benefits to consider?

- Does the policy list the correct owners?

- Are the beneficiary designations still accurate?

Retirement

When you include life insurance in your retirement plan, you want to make sure your policy is structured for growth or cash accumulation. In other words, your policy serves a dual purpose—death benefit protection and a possible nest egg or income stream for the insured if needed.

We recommend your plan contain more than life insurance. Diversification is the key to a successful retirement plan. For example, you might use life insurance instead of your 401(k) or IRA to supplement your retirement income. Or you might use life insurance in addition to your 401(k) or IRA. As we stated in Chapter 6, if you have an IRA, make sure your advisors have a proper understanding of the Required Minimum Distribution (RMD) rules.

Don't forget about Social Security. There are 2,728 rules and 567 ways to claim your Social Security, so which one do you choose when the Social Security Administration office is not allowed to give recommendations or assist you to maximize your benefits? We've talked about the benefits of waiting as long as possible before you start collecting your Social Security, but there are times it might make sense to begin collecting benefits before you're 70 years of age. Believe it or not, Social Security might just be your best growth opportunity in some situations.

One of the main difficulties of retirement planning is that so many factors must be considered, including interest rates, inflation, expected rates of return, life expectancy. Small changes in any of these factors can have a major impact on your financial security, which is why we strongly recommend that you consult with our experienced advisors using the latest in software to calculate how much you'll need for retirement and the options that you have.

Here's a high-level overview of a few major retirement planning options:

Benefits of Traditional and Roth IRAs

Roth or traditional IRAs can be an important part of your retirement plan. So you want to select the plan that works for you. The chart on the facing page illustrates key features of each plan.

Traditional IRA versus Roth IRA

FEATURE	TRADITIONAL IRA	ROTH IRA
Contributions	Can deduct contributions from your gross income.	Contributions will not be deducted from your income tax.
Investment growth	Investment gains are tax-deferred, meaning you can reinvest full amount of gains, helping your account to grow faster.	Investment gains are tax-deferred, meaning you can reinvest full amount of gains, helping your account to grow faster.
Taxable distributions	You pay taxes when you take the money out, which means there's a chance you may be in a higher tax bracket than when you made the contribution.	You can withdraw all qualified distributions tax-free. Withdrawals are not treated as additional income.
Required distributions	You can't avoid taxes by leaving the money in your traditional IRA indefinitely. Instead, beginning in the year you turn 70½, you must start withdrawing a minimum amount each year, even if you don't need it.	• You're not required to make withdrawals, even after the age of 70½. If you can get by without making withdrawals, then you can keep the money in your account for as long as you like. • Distributions can be inherited. Qualified beneficiaries can make withdrawals after your death.
Early withdrawal penalties	If you withdraw money before you turn 59½, you'll have to pay an extra 10% tax penalty, unless you qualify for an early withdrawal exception.	You can withdraw your contributions (not any gain) anytime, with no tax or penalty.

You might want to talk with your advisor about applying for a stretch IRA, where you can extend the financial life of either plan to a future generation.

Benefits of a 401(k)

Including a 401(k) in your retirement plan may or may not be the best option for you. If your employer matches contributions, we highly recommend contributing to your company's 401(k). If you contribute to a 401(k), you want to make sure your 401(k) administrator conducts an independent review of your 401(k) plan. They should provide you with a concise, customized written synopsis of your review. They should also provide a fund-allocation chart based on stated goals, age, and risk assessment.

Pros and Cons of a 401(k)

FEATURE	PROS	CONS
Contribution limits	Much higher than IRAs	—
Deductible contributions	Like IRAs, you can deduct contributions from your gross income.	—
Tax-sheltered growth	Investment gains are tax-deferred, meaning you can reinvest the full amount of gains, helping your account to grow faster.	—
Taxable distributions	—	You have to pay taxes when you take the money out, which means you may be in a higher tax bracket than when you made the contribution.
Required distributions	—	You can't avoid taxes by leaving the money in your traditional IRA indefinitely. Instead, beginning in the year you turn 70½, you must start withdrawing a minimum amount each year, even if you don't need it.
Early withdrawal penalties	—	If you withdraw funds before you turn 59½, you'll have to pay an extra 10% tax penalty unless you qualify for an early withdrawal exception.
Waiting periods	—	There's usually a waiting period before you can initiate a 401(k) plan with an employer, often it's between 6 months to 1 year.

Benefits of Retirement Plan Life Insurance Policies

Life insurance policies are a key component of your retirement plan and offer many options to protect your family and to provide an income after you retire.

Pros and Cons of Retirement Plan Life Insurance Policies

FEATURE	PROS	CONS
Investment returns	Modest, but guaranteed growth on cash value. Builds cash value that you can borrow against or withdraw.	—
Premiums	—	More expensive than others
Costs	—	Higher commissions and fees

As always, weigh the pros and cons, and then work with your financial advisor to create a plan that's customized to fit your financial situation and your retirement needs. And remember, life doesn't always work out as planned, so we strongly suggest scheduling annual meetings with your financial advisor to review the general state of your investments and how they still relate to your current plans.

Life Planning

Life insurance is a great way to help with taxes. Most effective life planning strategies involve life insurance in some way or another to assist with asset liquidity, debt repayment, income replacement, and even wealth accumulation. Most of the life insurance products outlined in this chapter are ideal for helping you decide how and to whom to leave what you own—your house, car, bank accounts, furniture, and life insurance, and anything else you personally own.

To create an effective plan for leaving your assets to others, contact a professional financial advisor. Some of the things you should discuss are:

- **Having a will in place.** The government will decide how your assets are distributed without one, which may not be what you or your loved ones want.

- **Knowing the net value of your assets.** If your assets exceed the exemption, your beneficiaries will be required to pay taxes.

- **Marital deduction.** Spouses are able to pass all assets to each other without tax consequences. However, the surviving spouse will amass a higher tax bill.

- **Taking advantage of the annual gift tax exclusion.** This minimizes future costs to your family in the event of your death. Currently, the maximum is $14,000 per year and can be given to an unlimited number of people.

- **Consider final expense insurance.** This insurance specifically covers the costs of burial and funeral, which in 2012 averaged over $8,000.[1] Although term and whole life policies can cover these last expenses, those who have provided for their loved ones with non-traditional means can benefit from this type of insurance by providing a safety net to cover these costs. These policies can be issued on a term or whole life basis.

Survivorship Life Insurance

In addition to the life insurance policies mentioned so far in this chapter, a *survivorship life insurance policy can be beneficial. This policy is a joint policy, where both you and your spouse are insured.* The death benefit is paid upon the second death—that is, with second-to-die survivorship; no death benefit is paid until both spouses are deceased. Second-to-die policies are commonly used to create a pool of funds to pay taxes and other expenses due at the death of the second spouse. Joint and survivorship policies are generally available under any type of permanent life insurance. Other than the fact that two people are insured under one policy, the policy characteristics remain the same.

Gifting "Outside the Box"

Grandparents have an opportunity to leave a legacy to their grandchildren through the gift of permanent life insurance; permanent life insurance can provide a safety net of financial security and provide protection in a way no other financial instrument can. A cash value permanent life insurance policy can last a lifetime and be an important part of a grandchild's financial future. Taking a closer look at the long-term benefits to the grandchild makes it clear why this financial instrument is a worthwhile option.

Some advantages of purchasing life insurance on a young child include:

- Your grandchild is guaranteed the ability to have permanent life insurance protection for his or her future family regardless of any changes in health down the road.

- It's a low-risk way of creating a financial asset which will grow tax-free.

- It can be a financial resource that can be used to help pay education expenses without affecting eligibility for financial aid.

- It's a source of cash value which can be accessed for anything a grandchild may need in the future, such as a first car, wedding, down payment on a first home, or even starting a business.

In many cases, grandparents take out a permanent life insurance policy on their grandchild and name themselves or the parent as owner and beneficiary and pay the premium each year. This approach gives full control of the policy and the option to eventually transfer ownership of the policy to the grandchild after he or she becomes an adult.

Charitable Giving

Life insurance is often used in conjunction with charitable giving as a means of amplifying the support you can provide to causes you believe in.

What Are Charitable Gifts of Life Insurance?

There's a common misconception about why people give to charity. Many people think it's because of the tax deduction the IRS and state governments allow. There must be something more basic at work than tax savings. The tax deduction doesn't eliminate the cost of charitable giving, it only reduces it. Studies of philanthropic behavior show that the most important reason why people give is their commitment to the mission and the specific programs of an organization. Every other reason, including tax incentives, is secondary to the importance of philanthropic motives. The personal satisfaction of supporting worthwhile causes drives charitable giving.

A gift of life insurance to a charity may allow you to make a substantial gift in a cost-effective way.

You have three basic options when making a charitable gift of life insurance:

- **You can transfer an existing policy to a charity,** in which case all incidents of ownership should be assigned to the charity, and the charity named as policy beneficiary.

- **You can apply for a new policy on your life,** with the charity named as the original policy owner and beneficiary, subject to state insurable interest laws.

■ **You can designate a charity as the beneficiary of an existing policy** that you continue to own, as long as no income tax advantages are sought (the gift of the proceeds to charity qualifies for a tax deduction on your assets).

Tax Facts

If you give $1,000 to charity, and your top marginal tax rate is 39.6 percent, you can save $396 in taxes. You still have to part with $604, even when the full effect of the tax deduction is figured in. Of course, in the lower brackets, the tax incentive is less. And there are limits on the amounts you may deduct in any one year based on your adjusted gross income.

Tax considerations become important in charitable giving when the goal is to (a) motivate the marginal giver—the person who needs a little "push" to make a financial commitment to an organization—and (b) to potentially increase the size of a donor's gift.

How Charitable Gifts Work

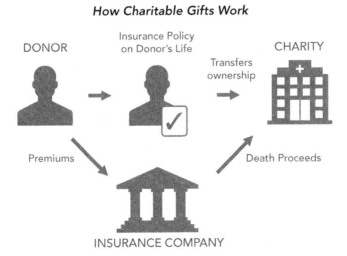

A donor transfers ownership of a life insurance policy to a charity, which changes the beneficiary designation to itself.

Often, the donor also pays the premiums on the policy, as shown above. Alternatively, a donor may make annual cash transfers to charity, which then uses the money to pay the premiums.

At the donor's death, the life insurance company pays the death benefit proceeds to the charity.

Example

Let's say you purchased a policy a number of years ago and you've paid annual premiums of $1,200 per year. Dividends on the policy have amounted to $3,600, which were paid to you in cash. You give the policy to charity exactly 12 years after the purchase date when it has a cash surrender value of $11,500. The net cost of the policy is $10,800 (total premiums of $14,400 minus dividends of $3,600). The net cost is less than the cash-surrender value, so $10,800 is the amount that you can use for a charitable contribution.

In the case of variable or variable-universal policies in which the policy owner has made wise choices and enjoyed positive returns, the cash value may be far greater than the total net premiums paid. Here, a donor's deduction is limited to the policy's basis—even though the charity could surrender the policy immediately for its much higher cash value.

Long-Term Care/Chronic Illness

You can buy long-term care insurance or a universal life or whole life insurance policy with a living benefits rider that can include benefits for long-term care, critical illness, or chronic illness. Here's an overview of each.

- **Long-term care insurance** helps to pay for an insured's chronic illnesses. It can be purchased as a stand-alone policy or as a rider attached to a life insurance product.

- **Universal or whole life insurance can be purchased with a long-term care rider or with living benefits or chronic illness riders.** These riders allow the insured to accelerate a portion of their life insurance policy's death benefit if the insured becomes chronically ill. Whatever death benefit isn't used goes to the insured's loved ones. These types of policies give the insured peace of mind by satisfying dual needs, if needed, into one product. Some of these riders come with a cost, and some don't, unless the rider is accessed.

Discuss your options with your financial advisor to determine which one is right for you.

Business Planning

We know this book isn't aimed at business owners, but in case you do own a business, we wanted to include information for you about how to protect it. Here are three types of business insurance to check into: cross-purchase/buy-sell agreements, key man, and executive bonus arrangements.

Cross-Purchase/Buy-Sell Agreements

Cross-purchase agreements (the most common type of buy-sell agreements) provide a greater certainty that a small business can continue after the death of one of the owners. Cross-purchase agreements:

- Allow parties to purchase a deceased business owner's interest at a certain price, and another party—typically the deceased owner's beneficiaries—to sell the interest at that price.

- Generally provide that each surviving owner's interest in the business remains the same in relation to the other owners, so if the relationships are unequal, they remain unequal after the death.

- Give business owners a certainty about who will purchase a deceased owner's interest, what the price will be, when the sale will take place, and where the funds will come from. If all goes well, the deceased's family gets a sum of cash they can use to help sustain them after his or her death, and the company has ensured its continuity.

Tax Facts

The premiums each owner personally pays are not tax-deductible. If, on the other hand, a corporation pays the premiums, they may be used as a deductible expense if they will be treated as compensation to the employees on whose behalf they are paid. The policy owners can use the proceeds to buy the deceased owner's interest, which allows the surviving owners to receive tax benefits.

Is a Cross-Purchase Agreement for You?

A cross-purchase agreement funded by life insurance can be an invaluable tool in helping business owners to establish a price for their business interest, and to ensure that both a buyer and the money to purchase that interest will be there when the need arises. Choosing the type of agreement depends on the business type and the owner's wishes.

Key Man Insurance

The purpose of key man insurance is to help protect a business from the economic losses or even failure that can occur when a key employee dies. Many businesses have crucial employees who are critical to the overall success and profitability of the business. Key employee insurance is life insurance owned by a business on the life of a key employee, which helps reimburse the business for the economic loss caused by the death of the employee.

Tax Facts

While premiums are not tax-deductible to the company, the death proceeds are commonly exempt from federal income tax if certain IRS requirements have been met. The tax consequences can be complex, so make sure to consult with your tax expert before making decisions.

Is Key Man Insurance for You?

Key man insurance can be vital to the continued survival and success of a small business. Take some time to look at your business and think about who is irreplaceable in the short term and what the economic consequences might be if they were suddenly not there.

Executive Bonus Arrangement

With an executive bonus arrangement, a business can use tax-deductible company funds to selectively provide valued benefits to key people. The benefits can include life insurance or disability policies where the employee applies for and owns the policy with the death benefits plus cash value accumulations passing to the employee or to their heirs, but the company pays the premiums. This is not the same as key man insurance, which is intended to protect the business from losses resulting from an employee's death. Rather, this is a way for the company to benefit the selected employee.

Tax Facts

The cash bonus or premium (either the premium or the premium plus applicable taxes) must be declared as additional compensation on the employee's

W-2. Eventually, the policy's annual cash value increase can exceed the tax on the bonus and may be borrowed or withdrawn to pay taxes.

Is an Executive Bonus Arrangement for You?

An executive benefit plan, when used effectively, can be a valuable tool to attract and retain key executives. If you have your own business, we strongly suggest you consult with your advisor about how using life insurance strategies can protect your company against property damage, liability, your death or your partner's death, workers' comp, data breach, and other situations that can harm your business.

KEY POINTS

- Review the options in this chapter, then talk to your financial advisor or agent about the insurance solutions that are best for your retirement plan.

- Develop a retirement plan you can live with and then review it regularly to make sure it meets your current situation.

NEXT STEPS

AS WE CONCLUDE THIS BOOK, we hope you have a solid grasp of the enormity of America's financial crisis, as well as a few ideas about how to start making changes in your life to avoid finding yourself in a dire situation, so that you don't embark on the longest vacation of your life without a plane ticket or a hotel booking.

It's our hope that you take the information we've offered, review the solutions, and meet with qualified life insurance professionals for an informed discussion about a retirement plan that's best for you and your family. But please note this important point: as a consumer, it's extremely important that you do your homework and choose the type of insurance advisor— and not the insurance carrier—who meets the needs of you and your family. To help you choose the right advisor, ask questions such as which insurance carriers the advisor represents, what products the carriers offer, and how often the advisor conducts policy reviews. You can also request references from the insurance advisor. Don't forget to ask your advisor about the online healthcare alternative we mentioned in Chapter 2.

After you decide on an advisor and a plan, we strongly suggest scheduling annual meetings with your advisor or advisors to review the general state of your retirement assets and how they still relate to your current plans. We want to stress again how imperative it is to review your insurance policies once a year. Products change and so do your needs, so you want to stay current.

Finally, we hope you feel a sense of empowerment and confidence that comes from knowledge and the belief that you can do this. Together with your financial advisor, you can make a plan to secure your future. As we've said, there are answers and you have options, so take heart. And start planning now so you can get on track, breathe deeply, and enjoy your retirement years with the peace that comes from knowing you and your loved ones are protected.

RETIREMENT INCOME WORKSHEET

Monthly Expenses

Place your current fixed monthly expenses in the chart below.

FIXED EXPENSES	DETAILS	MONTHLY AMOUNT
	Primary home mortgage/rent	$
	Utilities	$
Housing	Phone(s)	$
	Repairs/maintenance	$
	Other:	$
	Homeowners/renters	$
	Life insurance	$
	Health insurance	$
Insurance	Auto	$
	Disability	$
	Other:	$
	Vehicle payment(s)	$
	Fuel	$
Transportation	Repairs/maintenance	$
	Other:	$
	Food	$
	Clothing	$
Essentials	Co-payments/prescriptions/out-of-pocket expenses	$
	Other:	$
	Credit card payments	$
Debt Payments	Loan(s)	$
	Income tax	$
Taxes	Property tax	$
	Other:	$
		$
Other		$
	Total fixed expenses	$

Place your other monthly expenses in the chart below.

EXPENSES	DETAILS	MONTHLY AMOUNT
Entertainment	Dining out	$
	Activities	$
	Club membership(s)	$
	Hobbies	$
	Cable/satellite/internet	$
	Books/magazines/DVDs	$
	Other:	$
Personal Care	Gym membership	$
	Professional service (hair, spa, etc.)	$
	Other:	$
Travel/Vacation		$
		$
		$
Other	Gifts	$
	Other:	$
	Total other expenses	$
	Total combined monthly expenses	$

Place this amount in box B

Retirement Income Sources

Place the amount of monthly retirement income you are expecting to receive from all sources in the chart below.

SOURCE	DETAILS	MONTHLY AMOUNT
Current Income		$ $
Savings Account		$ $
Social Security		$ $
Qualified Employer Sponsored Plans	401(k) Defined benefit	$ $ $
IRAs (Roth, Traditional, SEP, etc.)		$ $
Annuities	Fixed annuity Variable annuity	$ $
Other		$
	Total monthly income	$

Place this amount in box A

Review your retirement income scenario

Now that you've calculated your monthly expenses and expected income, enter them on the right to determine if an income gap exists.

Retirement income   A

If you find that you are uncomfortable with the difference between your retirement income and expenses listed in box C or there is a gap, consider contacting me to discuss your options and create a retirement strategy that meets your needs.

Retirement expenses   B

Difference   C

ENDNOTES

Chapter 1

1. Colby, Sandra L., and Jennifer M. Ortman. "The Baby Boom Cohort in the United States: 2012 to 2060." U.S. Census Bureau. May 1, 2014.

2. Helman, Greenwald & Associates, Ruth, Nevin Adams, J.D., EBRI, Craig Copeland, Ph.D., EBRI, and Jack VanDerhei, Ph.D., EBRI. "The 2014 Retirement Confidence Survey: Confidence Rebounds— for Those with Retirement Plans." Employee Benefit Research Institute (EBRI). March 1, 2014.

3. Society of Actuaries (SOA). "Key Findings and Issues: Longevity." 2011 Risks and Process of Retirement Survey Report. June 1, 2012.

4. Social Security Administration. "Social Security." Actuarial Life Table. January 1, 2010.

5. Employee Benefit Research Institute (EBRI). "FAQs about Benefits— Retirement Issues." Retirement Question 14. January 1, 2012.

6. Butrica, Barbara A., Howard M. Iams, Karen E. Smith, and Eric J. Toder. "The Disappearing Defined Benefit Pension and Its Potential Impact on the Retirement Incomes of Baby Boomers." Social Security Bulletin, Vol. 69 No. 3. January 1, 2010.

7. Towers Watson. "Automatic Enrollment in 401(k) Plans Now Dominates at Large Employers, Towers Watson Survey Finds." June 30, 2010. Web.

8. O'Connell, Brian. "More U.S. Firms Shutter 401(k)s, Matching Programs." TheStreet. May 2, 2013.

9. Ruffing, Kathy. "What the 2014 Trustees' Report Shows About Social Security." Center on Budget and Policy Priorities. August 13, 2014.

10. The Pew Charitable Trusts. "Retirement Security Across Generations: Are Americans Prepared for Their Golden Years?" May 16, 2013.

11. United States Government Accountability Office. "Unemployed Older Workers: Many Experience Challenges Regaining Employment and Face Reduced Retirement Security." Report to the Chairman, Special Committee on Aging, US Senate. April 1, 2012.

12. Goyer, Amy. "The MetLife Report on the Oldest Boomers." MetLife Mature Market Institute. May 1, 2013.

13. Board of Governors of the Federal Reserve System. "Federal Reserve Board Issues Report on the Economic Well-Being of U.S. Households." Press Release. August 7, 2014.

14. McCann, Laurie. "Age Discrimination Is Pervasive, Tough to Prove—And Even Tougher to Litigate." *Aging Today*. January 19, 2012.

Chapter 2

1. Bureau of Labor Statistics. "Average Annual Expenditures and Characteristics of All Consumer Units." Consumer Expenditure Survey 2006–2012. September 1, 2013.

2. Marketdata Enterprises. "U.S. Weight Loss Market Forecast to Hit $66 Billion in 2013." December 31, 2012.

3. "Video Games in the United States." Video Game Sales Wiki. January 1, 2014. Web.

4. "XFINITY TV." HBO® Channel On Demand. March 31, 2015. Web.

5. "XFINITY® TV from Comcast: Digital Cable TV Service." XFINITY® TV. March 31, 2015. Web.

6. Gunders, Dana. "Wasted: How America Is Losing Up to 40 Percent of Its Food from Farm to Fork to Landfill." NRDC Issue Paper. August 1, 2012.

7. Gunders, "Wasted."

8. "58% Eat At A Restaurant At Least Once A Week." Rasmussen Reports™. July 11, 2013.

9. "Special Issue: U.S. Beverage Results for 2013." *Beverage-Digest*. March 31, 2014.

10. "Profile of the U.S. Candy Industry - 2013." National Confectioners Association. January 1, 2014.

11. "Workonomix Survey 2013." *Accounting/Principals*. March 13, 2013.

12. "Driving Citation Statistics." Statistic Brain Research Institute. July 8, 2014.

13. "Personal Consumption Expenditures by Major Type of Product." U.S. Bureau of Economic Analysis (BEA). March 27, 2015.

14. Chen, Tim. "American Household Credit Card Debt Statistics: 2014 - NerdWallet." *NerdWallet Credit Card Blog.* December 1, 2014.

15. Harris Poll. "The 2014 Consumer Financial Literacy Survey." National Foundation for Credit Counseling. 2015.

16. "Ally Bank Survey Explores Consumer Sentiment on Bank Fees." Ally Bank. November 10, 2011.

17. UNLV Center for Gaming Research. "Nevada Gaming Revenues, 1984-2014: Calendar Year Revenues for Selected Reporting Areas." February 1, 2015.

18. Goff, Brian. "The $70 Billion Fantasy Football Market." *Forbes Sports Money.* August 13, 2013.

19. North American Association of State and Provincial Lotteries (NASPL). "Lottery Sales and Transfers." January 1, 2015.

20. "Flash Facts About Lightning." *National Geographic.* June 24, 2005.

21. "What Are The Odds of a Shark Attack?" International Wildlife Museum. 2015.

Chapter 4

1. Scholarship AMERICA. "Fast Facts on Education in America." February 1, 2014.

2. US Government Accountability Office. "Inability to Repay Student Loans May Affect Financial Security of a Small Percentage of Retirees." Testimony before the Special Committee on Aging, US Senate.

3. Schuh, Scott, and Joanna Stavins. "The 2011 and 2012 Surveys of Consumer Payment Choice." Federal Reserve Bank of Boston Research Data Reports. January 1, 2014.

4. Dowd, Casey. "Boomer Retirees Need a Hand Paying Down Debt." *Fox Business.* October 9, 2014.

5. "CIBC Poll: Short on Savings, Canada's 50-Somethings Plan to Retire at Age 63—and Keep Working." CNW Group, Ltd., August 20, 2012.

6. Gustke, Constance. "Dying with Debt: Will Your Children Inherit Your Obligations?" *CardRatings.* March 18, 2013.

7. Lee, Donghoon. "Household Debt and Credit: Student Debt." Federal Reserve Bank of New York. February 28, 2013.

8. "The National Report Card on Higher Education." Measuring Up 2008. 2008.

9. Traub, Amy. "In the Red: Older Americans and Credit Card Debt." Middle Class Security Project: An Initiative of the AARP Public Policy Institute. 2013.

10. "Are Your Employees Borrowing from Their Futures?" TIAA-CREF Financial Services. June 18, 2014.

Chapter 5

1. "Quick Statistics on Deafness." National Institute on Deafness and Other Communication Disorders. October 3, 2014.

2. "Vision Impact Institute Releases Study on Corrective Lens Wearers in the U.S." Vision Impact Institute. 2014.

3. Gellar, Michelle, and Daniel Alter. "Dentures, A Matter of Health." *Inside Dental Technology*. August 1, 2013.

4. Social Security Advisory Board. "The Unsustainable Cost of Health Care." September 1, 2009.

5. "The Unsustainable Cost of Health Care."

6. "Key Cuts to Healthcare Waste Saves $3.6 Trillion." *Reuters*. June 14, 2010.

7. "Historic National Health Expenditure Data." Centers for Medicare & Medicaid Services, Office of the Actuary. 2013.

8. "Historic National Health Expenditure Data."

9. Johnson, Richard W., and Rudolph G. Penner. "Will Health Care Costs Erode Retirement Security?" Center for Retirement Research at Boston College. October 1, 2004.

10. "PR Tufts CSDD 2014 Cost Study." Tufts Center for the Study of Drug Development. November 18, 2014.

11. "The Hidden Epidemic: Finding a Cure for Unfilled Prescriptions and Missed Doses." *BCG/Focus*. December 1, 2003.

12. "Chronic Diseases and Health Promotion." Centers for Disease Control and Prevention. May 9, 2014.

13. "Chronic Diseases and Health Promotion."

14. "Chronic Diseases and Health Promotion."

15. "Projections of Future Growth of the Older Population." Administration on Aging (AoA). December 31, 2010.

16. "2014 Annual Report of the Boards of Trustees of the Federal Hospital Insurance and Federal Supplementary Medical Insurance Trust Funds." Centers for Medicare and Medicaid Services. July 28, 2014.

17. "The Facts on Medicare Spending and Financing: Overview of Medicare Spending." The Henry J. Kaiser Family Foundation. July 24, 2014.

18. "2014 Annual Report." Centers for Medicare and Medicaid Services.

19. Blendon, Sc.D., Robert J., and John M. Benson, M.A. "The Public and the Conflict over Future Medicare Spending." *New England Journal of Medicine.* September 12, 2013.

20. Houser, Ari. "Women & Long-Term Care." AARP Public Policy Institute. April 1, 2007.

21. "How Much Care Will You Need?" Long-Term Care Information. United States Department of Health and Human Services (USDHHS).

22. "Home Care Providers, Adult Day Health Care Facilities, Assisted Living Facilities and Nursing Homes." Genworth 2014 Cost of Care Survey. 2014.

Chapter 7

1. "Final Expense Life Insurance." *Final Expense Insurance.* Transamerica, 2011. Web.

GLOSSARY

401(K): a qualified retirement plan established by employers to which eligible employees may make salary deferral (salary reduction) before- or after-tax contributions. Employers offering a 401(k) plan may make matching or non-elective contributions (a predetermined percentage—for example 2 percent of an employee's salary) to the plan on behalf of eligible employees and may also add a profit-sharing feature to the plan. Earnings accrue on a tax-deferred basis.

401(K) LOAN: the ability to borrow amounts from a 401(k) fund with some restrictions: borrowing limits; loan length restrictions; lost investment growth; negative tax impact; outstanding loans at employment end causing potential taxes and penalties.

403(B): a type of defined contribution retirement plan that may be offered to employees of government and tax-exempt groups, such as schools, hospitals, and churches. Employees who are eligible can defer money from their paychecks into their 403(b) accounts, which work the same way as 401(k) plans.

ACCRUED EQUITY: the money value of a property or of an interest in a property (money put toward a property) in excess of claims or debts against it.

ASSISTED LIVING: housing for elderly or disabled people that provides nursing care, housekeeping, and prepared meals as needed.

BENEFICIARY: the person, people, or entity designated to receive the death benefits from a life insurance policy or annuity contract.

CAPITAL GAINS TAX: a tax levied on the profits that a person realizes when the sales price of a property or asset is higher than the purchase price.

CARRIER: a company or health maintenance organization (HMO) that provides healthcare coverage.

CASH VALUE: the amount of money the life insurance policy owner will receive as a refund if the policy owner cancels the coverage and returns the policy to the company. Also called "cash surrender value."

CHRONIC CONDITIONS: long-lasting conditions that can be controlled but not cured. The Centers for Disease Control (CDC) describes chronic disease as the leading cause of death and disability in the United States.

CLAIMANT: a person who believes that he or she has a right to something (such as an amount of money).

CONTRIBUTIONS: the amount you—and often your employer—contribute, or add to, an IRA or 401(k).

DEATH BENEFIT: amount paid to the beneficiary upon the death of the insured.

DEFERRED TAX: earnings resulting from interest, dividends, or capital gains that accumulate tax-free until the person withdraws and takes possession of them. A Traditional IRA is one of the most common types of tax-deferred retirement plans.

EQUITY: the money value of a property or of an interest in a property in excess of claims or debts against it.

HOME EQUITY LOAN: a type of loan in which the borrower uses the equity of his or her home as collateral. Home equity loans are often used to finance major expenses such as home repairs, medical bills, or college education.

HOMEOWNERS ASSOCIATION: an organization in a subdivision, planned community, or condominium that makes and enforces rules for the properties in its jurisdiction.

INDEXES: in economics and finance, a statistical measure of changes in a representative group of data points. Examples are the Consumer Price Index, stock market indexes (such as NASDAQ and Dow Jones), and job indexes (such as unemployment rates, hours worked, average income).

INSURANCE PREMIUMS: the cost of obtaining insurance coverage; paid by the insured as a lump sum or in installments during the duration of the policy.

INSURED: the person or organization covered by an insurance policy.

LINE OF CREDIT: an amount of credit extended to a borrower.

LONG-TERM CARE: a range of services and supports that may be needed to meet someone's personal care needs. Most long-term care is not medical care; it's assistance with the basic personal tasks of everyday life, sometimes called Activities of Daily Living (ADLs). Long-term care services can include traditional medical services, social services, and housing.

LONG-TERM CARE BENEFITS: coverage that provides help for people when they are unable to care for themselves because of prolonged illness or disability. Benefits are triggered by specific findings of "cognitive impairment" or inability to perform certain actions known as "Activities of Daily Living." Benefits can range from help with daily activities while recuperating at home to skilled nursing care provided in a nursing home.

LONG-TERM DISABILITY INSURANCE: insurance that offers income protection to individuals who become disabled for a long period of time, and as a result can no longer work during that time period.

LUMP-SUM PAYMENT: a single payment of money, as opposed to a series of payments made over time.

MANDATORY WITHDRAWAL: the amount that traditional, SEP, and simple IRA owners and qualified plan participants must begin withdrawing from their retirement accounts by April 1 following the year they reach age 70½ years of age. Commonly known as Required Minimum Distribution (RMD).

MATCHING CONTRIBUTIONS: amounts contributed by an employer to the retirement savings account of an employee who makes a similar contribution, usually to a 401(k) plan. These are contributions made by a company in addition to and conditional upon the salary deferral contributions made by the participating employee. Generally, the employer's contribution may match the employee's elective contribution up to a certain dollar amount or percentage of compensation.

MEDICAID: a US government program, financed by federal, state, and local funds, of hospitalization and medical insurance for persons of all ages within certain income limits.

MEDICARE: a US government program of hospitalization insurance and voluntary medical insurance for persons aged 65 and over and for certain disabled persons under 65.

MORTGAGE: a legal agreement in which a person borrows money to buy property (such as a house) and pays back the money over a period of years.

NONPARTICIPATING POLICY: a life insurance policy that does not grant the policy owner the right to policy dividends.

NURSING HOME: a private institution providing residential accommodations with healthcare, especially for elderly people.

PAID-UP: an event occurring when a life insurance policy will not require any further premiums to keep the coverage in force.

PAID-UP ADDITIONS: additional amounts of life insurance purchased using dividends; these insurance amounts require no further premium payments.

PENSIONS: a fixed sum to be paid regularly to a person, typically following retirement, typically based on contributions made by an employer to funds set aside for an employee's future benefit. In defined-benefit plans, the employer guarantees that the employee will receive a definite amount of benefit upon retirement, regardless of the performance of the underlying investment pool. In defined-contribution plans, the employer makes predefined contributions for the employee, but the final amount of benefit received by the employee depends on the investment's performance.

POLICY: the contract issued by the insurance company to the insured.

PREMIUM: the amount paid by the insured to an insurance company to obtain or maintain an insurance policy.

PROVISIONAL INCOME: the level of income that is used to determine whether a taxpayer is liable for tax on their Social Security benefits, and by how much. Provisional income is calculated by making certain adjustments to the taxpayer's gross income. Provisional income = gross income + tax-free interest + 50 percent of Social Security benefits + any tax-free fringe benefits and exclusions - adjustments to income (except for the student loan deduction, tuition and fees deduction, or domestic production-activities deduction).

REGULAR INSTALLMENTS: consistent periodic payments, usually monthly, of a debt. Often includes interest and a portion of the principal.

REQUIRED MAXIMUM DISTRIBUTION (RMD): amounts the US federal government requires you to withdraw annually from traditional IRAs and employer-sponsored retirement plans.

REVERSE MORTGAGE: a type of loan available to homeowners, 62 years or older, which allows them to convert part of their accrued equity in their home into cash.

ROTH IRA: an individual retirement plan that has many similarities to the traditional IRA, but contributions are not tax-deductible and qualified distributions are tax-free. Similar to other retirement plan accounts, non-qualified distributions from a Roth IRA may be subject to a penalty upon withdrawal.

SEP IRA: a variation of the traditional Individual Retirement Account (IRA) that can be used by small business owners to provide retirement benefits for themselves and their employees with no significant administration costs.

SINGLE PREMIUM WHOLE LIFE POLICY: a type of limited-payment policy that requires only one premium payment.

STRETCH IRA: an option that allows you to extend the financial life of an IRA to a future generation. It can be applied to both traditional and Roth IRAs. This allows an IRA owner to pass on assets to a designated second-generation or even a third- or fourth-generation beneficiary while allowing them to enjoy the benefits of tax-deferred and/or tax-free growth as long as possible.

TAX BENEFITS: an allowable deduction on a tax return intended to reduce a taxpayer's liability.

TRADITIONAL IRA: an individual retirement account (IRA) that allows individuals to direct pretax income, up to specific annual limits, toward a retirement fund that can grow tax-deferred (no capital gains or dividend income is taxed). Non-qualified distributions from an IRA may be subject to a penalty upon withdrawal.

RESOURCES

HEALTH INSURANCE NEEDS: Learn about finding and paying for health insurance, including Medicare and Medicaid.

www.usa.gov/health-insurance

LIFE HAPPENS: Learn about which type of insurance is best for you. Life Happens is a nonprofit organization dedicated to helping Americans take personal financial responsibility through the ownership of life insurance and related products, including disability and long-term care insurance:

www.lifehappens.org/

LIFE INSURANCE NEEDS ANALYSIS: Calculate life insurance coverage needs using this online calculator:

www.lifehappens.org/insurance-overview/life-insurance/calculate-your-needs/

LONG-TERM CARE INFORMATION: The American Association for Long-Term Care Insurance provides links to assist you in your search for information related to long-term care and LTC insurance.

www.aaltci.org/long-term-care-insurance/resource-center/

SOCIAL SECURITY ADMINISTRATION: Take some of the guesswork out of planning your future retirement. This Social Security planner page lists calculators you can use to figure your retirement and disability benefits and benefits for your survivors.

www.ssa.gov/planners/benefitcalculators.html

TOPCONSUMERREVIEWS.COM: If you find yourself struggling with debt, this site can direct you to reviewed resources that offer services and opportunities to reduce your burden.

www.topconsumerreviews.com/debt-relief-programs/
?src=top.xoom&gclid=CPzfrYWMn8cCFU2SfgodVBADMA

Acknowledgments

WE WOULD LIKE to specifically thank Kelly Malone, Jessie and Katie, Kirsten Leeds, John Phelps, Cheryl Daniels, Amy Jeffryes, Marisa Jackson, Bobbie Watkins, Casandra Burns, and Ken Ogan. Our gratitude also extends to anyone else we may have missed who helped us with this book by providing support, talking things over, reading, writing, offering comments, and allowing us to use their stories and names. We would also like to thank all who assisted in editing and/or proofreading.

About the Authors

BEGINNING AS AGENTS in the life insurance industry, husband and wife duo, David and Nancy Ellis realized the power of knowledge and trusting relationships. With these values at heart, they founded Life and Annuity Masters, a national life insurance organization that measures success by preparing people for their future, not simply by the bottom line. David and Nancy continue this mission with the release of their first book, America's Retirement Reality Check.

We'd love to hear from you!

If you've enjoyed this book, have more questions, comments, or need an insurance or financial assessment, visit us at:

Life and Annuity Masters:

www.LAAMINC.com

Women Empowering Financial Independence:

www.WEFlyourway.com

Coastal Private Wealth Management:

www.cpwminc.com

CPSIA information can be obtained
at www.ICGtesting.com
Printed in the USA
FSOW04n0152090116
15377FS